Simply Serging

Simply Serging

25 Fast and Easy Projects for Getting to Know Your Overlocker

Charlene Phillips

KRAUSE PUBLICATIONS
Cincinnati, Ohio

Contents

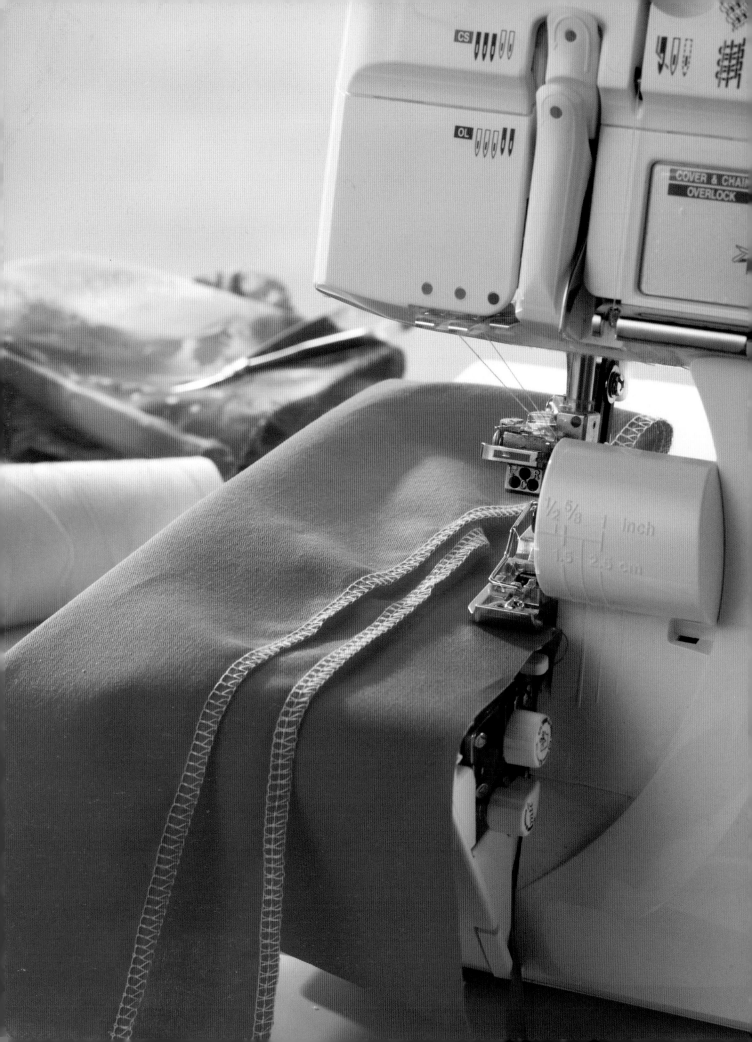

INTRODUCTION: WHY USE A SERGER?

A sewing machine is one of the most useful pieces of equipment a sewist can have. You have it mastered, and now you are ready to begin using the next best thing: a serger. The serger's function is to cut and finish an edge of material, providing a finished seam. Serging results in durable, high-quality, extremely *fast* stitches and edge finishes that are more desirable than sewing machine stitches for sewing garments, projects with exposed edges, and items that will endure lots of stress.

If you are new to using a serger, don't be intimidated by the machine itself. Instead of feeling anxious about threading all those cones, think instead of how creative you can get when you're able to use more than one color for your stitches.

Take it one step at a time. Pull out your serger's manual, and along with this book, you will have enough information to not only learn how to use your machine, but to complete many fabulous projects successfully. Instead of trying to learn a lot of techniques at once, or too many in one sitting, take it slow and enjoy every new skill—mastering one at a time. When you get a bit discouraged, take a short break (chocolate does

wonders!). Remember, we all start at one spot: the beginning.

Get to know your individual serger first. Begin by threading each looper and needle with a different thread color. If your machine has a color-coded thread path, choose colors to match. This will help you learn which part of the serger stitch is made by which part of the machine. Knowing this will save you time later when you need to make adjustments.

Grab some fabric from your scrap bag and start with the basic overlock stitch on cotton material; play with the tension, stitch length and stitch width (you'll learn more about these things later in the book). Watch the foot and cutting guide, and you will learn where the cutting action takes place. Watch your needle to see where the seam falls on the fabric edge. Mark some gentle curves on fabric and try to stitch along your mark. Then, move on to different fabric types and weights. Grab a spool or two of decorative thread and keep at it. The more you thread and rethread your serger, the more your confidence will grow.

Once you feel comfortable with the basic overlock stitch, move on to a rolled edge hem or a flatlock stitch. Ready to

tackle some special serger feet? Grab the cover stitch foot or the piping foot, more scraps, and serge away! This book will walk you through it all.

Before long, you will be creating all kinds of serged projects, from placemats to a zippered cosmetics case. You will be surprised how quickly each project stitches up using the serger. Once you begin using your serger to its fullest extent, and for more than just finishing seams, you will wonder what you ever did without one (and never want to give it up).

This book will provide you with many opportunities for practical serging and techniques to take your serging to the next step of decorative possibilities. Have fun while learning all your serger can do to make your sewing tasks so much more enjoyable.

Serger vs. overlocker: What's the difference?

The machine is the same; only the name for it varies depending on where you live. In the United States, the term *overlocker* has largely been replaced by *serger*. In other parts of the world, such as the UK and Australia, the term *overlocker* remains in use.

PART 1

GETTING TO KNOW YOUR SERGER

Household sergers have been around since the 1980s. Even though machine models may differ in how they look, or how many threads they use, they all share the same basic parts. The more familiar you are with your serger and its operations, the friendlier it will appear.

Serger Basics

A serger (or overlocker) makes sewing more efficient than ever before. Imagine the possibilities of stitching seams, trimming seam allowances, and finishing those seam edges all in one step! All your seams are finished with a very professional look that, with the serger, happens much faster than sewing the seam allowance and then going back and overcasting the same seam using your sewing machine.

As I familiarize you with the serger and its abilities, I will be addressing FAQs submitted to my website.

Sewing machine or serger?

Q: I would like to know when you absolutely have to use a serger. I have seen info that says you can use a twin needle on knits to duplicate the serger.
   –*Margaret Cherry, Long Beach, California*

A sewing machine can use a twin needle on knits to overcast or create a sporty hem; however, the serger does not require special needles or the use of a pintuck foot and will do the job much faster. If you are wanting to replicate the hems found on many knits and sportswear, you will want a machine capable of a cover stitch.

A serger is capable of adding embellishments, sewing various hem stitches, and creating decorative flatlock stitches to add unique details to your sewing projects. You can make one-of-a-kind garments using special threads such as metallic and decorative rayon, or ribbons.

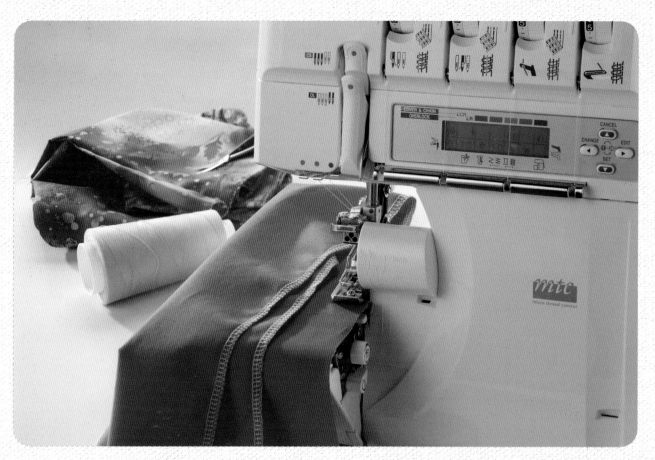

Serging suits many fabrics

Sergers are wonderful for stitching seams in swimwear and knit T-shirts. They create rolled hems that give you neat, narrow edges for hems and ruffles. Silk fabrics are easy to sew with pucker-free seams; cover stitching can be used as a decorative effect or to create a sporty look; and sweater knit seams are perfectly overcast and won't unravel.

Can a serger entirely take the place of your sewing machine? Not necessarily. A serger is normally thought of as merely a complement to your sewing machine. However, it can do so much more than just make an overlock stitch on straight seams. Take the time to think about "serger sewing." Begin thinking when it is best to use the serger and when to head for your sewing machine. You will find many projects can be completed with the serger alone, while other projects use both serger and sewing machine to achieve the best results.

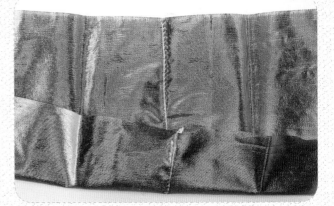

There are many projects that can be constructed from start to finish using the serger. Want to quickly sew a pair of pajama bottoms? Head to your serger for perfect construction form and save loads of sewing time. This is easily done when following the garment industry's method of "flat construction"—keeping the garment flat for as long as possible. Need a new set of napkins to jazz up your next meal? Grab some fabric, set the serger for a rolled edge hem, and make a matching set in less than an hour.

Make ribbing

The serger can be used to sew ribbing around the neckline, wrist, waist or ankles. For a designer cuff, set your serger for a 3- or 4-thread overlock stitch. Fold the cuff ribbing in half horizontally, so the greatest stretch is in the lengthwise direction. Fold the cuff once more in half, from top to bottom. Serge along the raw edge, through all four layers. Turn the top single layer of fabric back onto itself to complete the cuff. Attach the cuff to the sleeve using the serger.

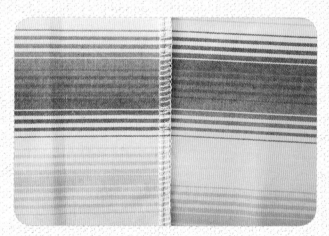

Easy matching

A simple technique will achieve perfectly matched stripes or plaids. Align the patterns by placing the fabrics right sides together, extending the bottom layer of fabric about ⅛" (3mm) to the right of the top layer. The extended fabric makes both layers visible so you can keep patterns aligned throughout the seam length.

Add an exposed zipper

For buttonholes, head for your sewing machine. The same for inserting invisible zippers. However, use your serger to add an exposed zipper to a project—such as this colorful pop of red on black fabric.

What to look for in a serger

Q: I don't have a serger (yet). But I am a person who likes to look into what I plan to buy so I know I'm getting something that fits my needs. How does someone like myself, who wants a serger in the future, know what to look for? What should I be looking for in a serger—in both lower-end and higher-end machines?

–Debra Jo Nail, Dresden, Tennessee

Q: I do not own a serger but would love to purchase one. I have no clue what to look for or how one works, much less what to use it for.

–Robin Hall, Riva, Maryland

Buying a serger can be confusing at times and a bit overwhelming. Take it one step at a time. Knowing what a serger does and all the stitches available on one can help guide you through the process. Before buying one, do some research, compare and test-drive a number of them.

There are many different types of sergers using two, three, four and five threads. Some very expensive "top-of-the-line" models have up to ten threads. Just remember that the more needles and number of threads, the more stitch types available to you.

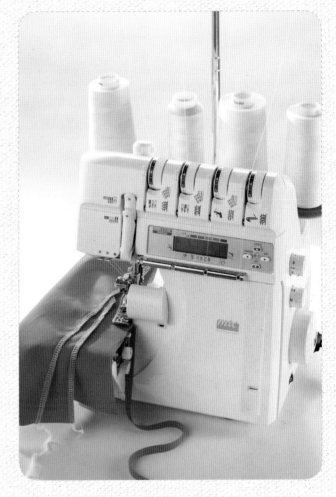

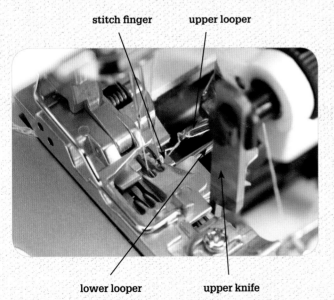

stitch finger   **upper looper**

lower looper   **upper knife**

How it works: The basic serger overlock stitch

The basic serger overlock stitch is made with *needles* and *loopers*. Stitches are formed around one or two stitch fingers (small prongs on the needle plate). *Loopers* are used instead of a bobbin to form the stitches. Looper threads do not penetrate the fabric. The *needles* stitch a straight seam line while the loopers interlock with the needle to form an overcasting stitch. Right before each stitch is made, the upper and lower knives cut the fabric, giving the fabric edges a clean and professional finish.

To summarize, the fabric is fed into the serger and first reaches the feed dogs, then is moved along as the knives cut the edge. The loopers and needles perform the stitches on the fabric. Lastly, the fabric is fed off the stitch fingers behind the needle.

As you begin to compare the many types of sergers, capabilities and options, it can be tough deciding which one to buy. To add to the confusion, each manufacturer names their serger machines differently. The machine may be called a 4/3/2 thread serger, or 2034XYZ. Doing a bit of homework, such as knowing the differences between 2-, 3-, 4- and 5-thread sergers and the stitches each serger is capable of, will make the task more manageable. Each needle and each looper must have a designated thread. So a 3-thread serger will have one needle and two loopers to equal three spools of thread. A 4-thread serger will have two needles and two loopers and equal four spools of thread. The more spools of thread you have, the more stitch types are available to you.

Q: How does one determine what type of serger would work best in their situation? What do I look for, what do I compare, and what concepts and ideas do I consider in choosing a machine, such as number of threads and abilities of the machine?
–V. Heins, Buhl, Idaho

First, list the stitches you want in a serger. Then list the serger models by the number of threads and the types of stitches each makes. Cross out the models that lack all the features and stitches you are looking for. Next, think about the various optional features you might wish to have. You will quickly see the thread number you should be looking for. For example, if you wish to use the cover stitch, you have narrowed the search down to a 5-thread serger. Now, start looking for a serger model with all the features you have listed, and then consider affordability. (For a sample comparison-shopping chart, see page 16.)

upper knife

lower knife

The serger's knives
A serger has two knives, upper and lower, which are the serger's cutting mechanism. The lower knife is stationary, while the upper moves in an up-and-down motion. They work similar to the action of scissors. When you first use your serger, the knives are automatically engaged for the cutting action on the basic overcast stitch. There are several stitches where both knives are disengaged, such as the cover stitch and the chainstitch.

Serger types and the stitches they perform

Sergers are constantly changing, so the following is by no means an exhaustive list of serger types, but it will give you a better understanding of serger "lingo." The first number (with the exception of the 2/3 serger) lets you know the maximum number of thread spools used. The numbers following indicate the versatility. For example, the 4/3/2 thread serger will make the 4-thread overlock, along with the 3-thread and the 2-thread overlock stitch. (The stitches themselves are shown and described individually on pages 18–21.)

✄ **2/3 or 3-thread serger:** Has one needle and upper and lower loopers; sews the 2-thread overlock, 3-thread overlock, flatlock stitch, and rolled edge stitch.

✄ **4/2 thread serger:** Has two needles and upper and chainstitch lower loopers; sews the 2-thread overlock, 2-thread chainstitch, 4-thread overlock, and flatlock stitch.

✄ **4/3/2 or 4/3 thread serger:** Has two needles and upper and lower loopers; sews the 2-thread overlock, 3-thread overlock, 4-thread overlock, flatlock, and rolled edge stitch.

✄ **5/4/3/2 thread serger:** Has two needles, upper and lower loopers, and chainstitch looper; sews 2-thread overlock, 3-thread overlock, 4-thread overlock, 5-thread overlock, flatlock stitch, rolled edge stitch, chainstitch, and cover stitch.

As you can see, all sergers do not create every overlock stitch. Decide which stitches are most important to you and your sewing. Then make yourself a serger shopping chart to begin comparing different makes and models.

What's the difference between a 3-thread and a 4-thread serger?

The number of threads determines the number and types of stitches a particular serger is capable of. For example, a 3-thread serger uses three threads and is a versatile machine, as you can seam, finish edges, and sew blind hems and rolled hems. On a 3-thread serger, the seams may not be as durable in stress areas, so you may want to head to your sewing machine as needed to reinforce these areas in the garment. Move a step up to a 4-thread serger, which has even more capabilities, since one more thread has been added to the stitches. When all four threads are used, it can create a 4-thread overlock with an added stitch (also called 4-thread with safety seam) for durability.

Serger comparison shopping chart

Make a shopping chart to help determine the best serger for you. List the features you want and eliminate the serger models that don't have your required features, narrowing down your options to the models that will fit your needs.

Stitches I wish to have:
rolled edge hem
flatlock
cover stitch
chainstitch

Serger model	Serger types	Serger stitches	Other features
~~xty~~	2/3 or 3-thread	2-thread and 3-thread overlock, flatlock, and rolled edge hem	
~~jwx~~	4/2 thread	2-thread and 4-thread overlock, 2-thread chainstitch, flatlock, and rolled edge hem	color-coded threading; easy convert to rolled edge
~~tgg~~	4/3/2 or 4/3 thread	2-thread, 3-thread, and 4-thread overlock, flatlock, and rolled edge hem	color-coded threading; easy convert to rolled edge; lessons available
twb ✓	5/4/3/2 thread	2-thread, 3-thread, 4-thread, and 5-thread overlock, flatlock, rolled edge hem, chainstitch, and cover stitch	color-coded threading; easy convert to rolled edge; has differential feed; lessons available; 3 extra feet

Q: What would be better for purse construction, a 3- or 4- thread overlock?
–Toni Sergent, Hamilton, Ohio

A 4-thread uses one more thread than the 3-thread, giving a stronger and more durable stitch. The serger stitch you use always depends on the size and purpose of your project, and in this case, possibly the weight the purse will be holding. If lining the purse, which gives it a double construction, you might be able to use the 3-thread. When choosing which serger stitch to use, consider fabric type, weight and the project you are stitching.

Additional considerations

Other design features of a serger model may also be important to you. Read through the questions below, and add those features you certainly want to have in a serger to your shopping chart. For example, do you wish to have a color-coded threading diagram handy? Then add it to your shopping chart, and only look at serger models that have that feature.

Additional design features to consider include:

- ✄ How easy is it to thread? Some machines have a color-coded threading diagram, making it easier to thread. Some may have parts that swing away for easier threading. There are others that are "jet-air," which thread almost automatically. Watch lint and dust buildup in these machines, so it doesn't become trapped in the air channels.
- ✄ Is it easy to change the tension?
- ✄ How many feet come with the machine? Which are optional? Which are most important to you?
- ✄ Does the serger take standard needles or special needles (which could be harder to find)?

- ✄ What are the various stitch options? Think of the types of stitches important to your sewing. Does the serger offer the stitches you need?
- ✄ Since the rolled edge is one of the most commonly used stitches, how easy is it to convert the serger to the rolled edge stitch?
- ✄ Does the machine have differential feed? With the many new types of fabrics, especially those with some stretch, having this option can make it easier to sew perfect stitches without distortion on knits and ribbing. Differential feed also allows gathering on lightweight to medium-weight fabrics.
- ✄ Does the upper knife disengage easily and without the use of tools?
- ✄ If buying from a dealer, does the shop offer lessons? How available is the repair service? What is the warranty?
- ✄ How much do you wish to spend? Naturally, there is a raise in cost the more options you have.

The types and number of stitches of various models on the market can change each year. It is best to look at each serger model you are thinking of buying, and jot down the number and types of stitches to compare each model. Remember, think about the types of stitches of each serger and those you will use most often. You don't want to be disappointed or overwhelmed.

Once you have chosen a serger, slowly learn its parts and all its capabilities. Keep the manual and this book close by. The best way to keep that serger out of the closet and from becoming hidden away is to practice, practice, practice! It is all up to you. Master one stitch and move on to the next. As you move through the projects in this book, master the basic principle, and then add to that skill using another variation of one of the tips scattered throughout.

Common stitches

The choice of stitch used on your project is based on the fabric, the use of the project, and whether the seam is located in a stress area. The most commonly used stitches are the 3-thread overlock, 4-thread overlock, and rolled hem. Your machine may also be capable of the flatlock stitch, cover stitch or the chainstitch.

For a narrower stitch
There are times you need the 3-thread overlock to be as narrow as possible. If your serger has two needles, remove the left needle and only use the right one.

3-thread overlock stitch
The stitch is formed using one needle and upper and lower loopers. It is used to finish seams that don't require lots of wear and tear. It is also suitable as a seam on stretchy fabrics such as knits and as a finished edge for raveling fabrics. Use the standard serger foot.

Making pintucks
Make pintucks using a 2- or 3-thread overlock. Put decorative thread in the looper(s) if desired. Mark each pintuck. Place the fold of the pintuck under the presser foot so that the right side of the pintuck faces up. Serge. Press pintucks in one direction.

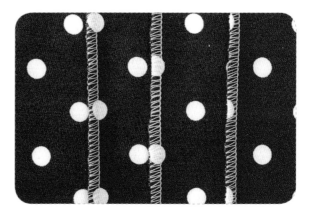

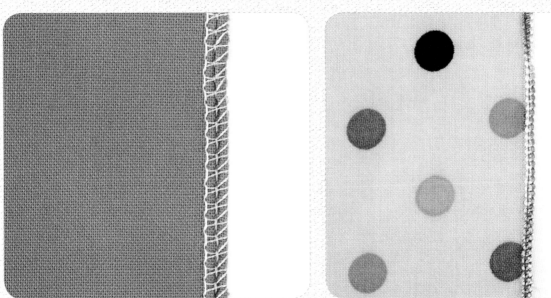

4-thread overlock stitch

This stitch is formed by using two needles and the upper and lower loopers. It provides a durable seam. Use the standard serger foot.

Rolled edge stitch

Use for narrow, and oftentimes decorative, hems. It is suitable for seams in lightweight fabrics. There are two types of rolled edge stitch: a 2-thread rolled edge stitch uses one needle and one looper, and a 3-thread rolled edge stitch uses one needle and both upper and lower loopers. The 3-thread uses more thread, and therefore can provide the most coverage. To add a decorative effect to your 3-thread rolled hem, use standard thread in the needle and the lower looper. Use decorative thread in the upper looper, as this is the one that will wrap around the edge. Use the standard serger foot.

Lettuce edge hem

Create a lettuce edge hem on knits by pulling the fabric slightly while stitching with a rolled edge hem stitch.

Tips

✄ To achieve a decorative edge hem that is reversible, place decorative thread in the upper and lower loopers.

✄ To make a more predominant rolled edge hem, stitch it twice, not cutting the second time.

Chainstitch

This stitch is made using one needle and one looper, usually called a dedicated chain looper. The top is made with the needle and looks like a straight stitch, while the bottom is a row of loops. If you wish to see the decorative loop side, always stitch on the wrong side of the fabric. Most machines require using the cover stitch foot and extension plate.

Cover stitch

The cover stitch is also called a flat joining seam. This stitch is made using one looper thread and two or three needles. The cover stitch appears as a double (or triple) row of topstitching on the right side of the fabric, and as an overlock stitch on the wrong side. This stitch is useful for hemming or topstitching. The underside stitch is also used as a decorative stitch, especially when adding specialty thread to the looper. The cover stitch foot has "floating toes" to help guide the fabric and to prevent any sideways movement when topstitching, binding edges, or attaching elastic. The upper knife is fully disengaged, as no cutting is used. Most machines require using the cover stitch foot and extension plate.

Chainstitch uses

A chainstitch can be used without fabric to make button loops, belt loops, or even to create "yarn" for tassels.

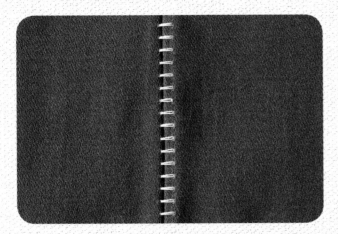

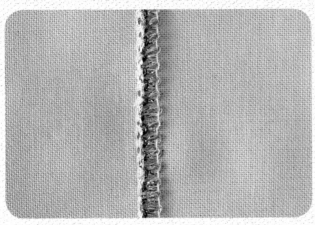

Q: How do you flatlock on a standard serger machine?
–*Catherine McAra, New Zealand*

Thread for a 2-, 3-, or 4-thread overlock. Loosen tensions on both the upper and lower loopers from 0 to 3. Loosen the needle(s) tension to 0. After serging, gently pull the thread seam apart to create the flatlock. Use two colors of decorative thread and a 3-thread overlock stitch for a unique design.

Add ribbon
Insert ribbon in between the "ladders" for a decorative touch.

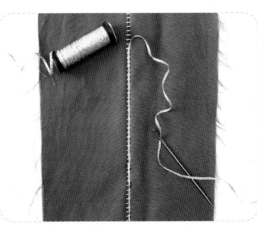

Flatlock stitch
This stitch is a serged seam that lies flat and can be made with two, three or four threads. The flatlock stitch can be used as a decorative feature or a purely functional seam. Functional uses include serging a seam in bulky fabrics that don't ravel, or when piecing together a quilt. The stitch can be used to add a decorative effect, as one side creates a "ladder." When the seam is pulled open to lay flat, the stitches resemble rungs on a ladder, while the opposite side shows loops. Use the standard serger foot.

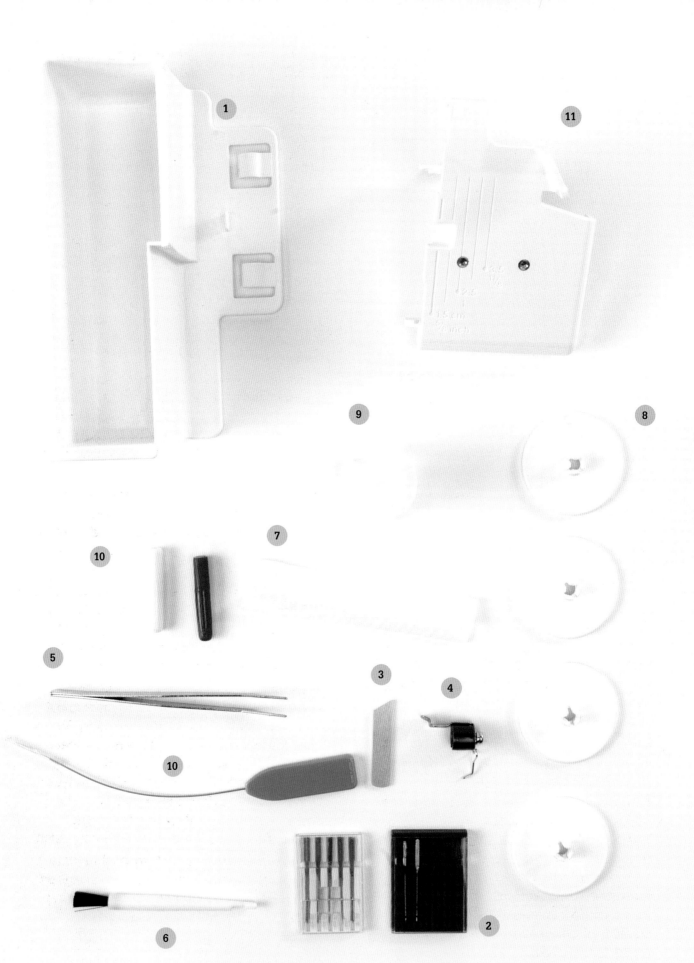

Materials, Accessories and Other Necessities

Most sergers come with an accessory kit, and the contents will vary depending on the machine model. Lay out your accessories and grab your manual to identify what you have and what each is for. Each one is intended to make certain tasks easier.

1. Waste catcher. The serger creates lots of waste as it trims the fabric edge. Most models have a waste catcher that attaches to the front of the machine to collect the waste as it falls away. If you find the machine's waste catcher too small, make your own (see instructions on page 114).

2. Needles. Some sergers use one needle, while others have two or three. Choose your serger needles by fabric type, just as you do for a conventional sewing machine. The universal needle is the most commonly used. However, choose appropriately based on your fabric and reason for the stitch. For example, top stitch needles accommodate heavy metallic, and ballpoint needles are used with knits and synthetic materials.

Most sergers use standard household sewing needles of system 130/705H. For best results use size 70/10, 80/12, or 90/14. It is important never to use a needle larger than size 90/14 on your serger, as a larger size will interfere with the looper action. When not using a needle position, it is best to remove the needle and tighten the needle screws.

3. Knife. Most sergers come with an extra lower knife; some may include both upper and lower replacements. The lower knife is usually included, as it tends to wear out faster than the upper.

4. Upper looper converter. Your serger may need a converter for serging a 2-thread stitch. This converter is to bypass the upper looper. The converter is placed on top of the upper looper arm and clicked in place. (Check your manual to properly install.) Before beginning to stitch, turn the handwheel to ensure that the converter is correctly mounted and the threads are forming a proper thread chain.

5. Tweezers. Special serger tweezers are long and angled for inserting threads in small places where your fingers can't readily reach. They are especially useful when threading looper guides and needles.

6. Lint brush/needle inserter. Most manufacturers supply you with a brush/needle inserter in one handy tool. The lint brush is crucial to reaching those small places to remove dust and fluff. The other end is a needle inserter with a small hole in the tip to make quick and easy work of inserting your needles.

7. Nets. When placed over thread spools, a net will prevent the thread from unraveling and twisting, allowing the thread to flow smoothly from the thread spool. Nets are especially useful on stretchy woolly nylon, rayons, and monofilament nylon thread.

8. Spool caps. Spool caps are necessary when using conventional thread spools, to allow a smooth, even feed of the thread. They also keep the spool from "jumping" and the thread from catching on slits or burrs on the spool.

9. Coneholders. Coneholders are used with cone thread to prevent rattling while serging. The cone thread has a much wider base and needs to be properly stabilized. Place the coneholder on the thread stand and the cone thread over it.

10. Threaders. There are various types of looper and needle threaders on the market, but they are definitely a very helpful accessory. To thread the loopers, use a looper threader that is a long 6" (15cm) wire with an eye large enough to accommodate all thread types. Another type of threader is a needle threader, which can be extremely useful when threading the serger needles with textured yarns such as woolly nylon.

11. Cover stitch/chainstitch extension plate. In order to cover stitch or chainstitch, an extension plate is normally necessary to cover the cutting blades.

Q: How often should I replace the knife of my serger?
                —*Linda Rodriguez, Sunrise, Florida*

When you start noticing jagged cut edges, it's time to change the knife. Keeping one on hand ensures you are always ready to sew. (See page 135 for more on changing the knives.)

All about needles

✂ Keep a good needle in your serger. Dull and bent needles cause stitch problems. A blunt needle won't sufficiently pierce the fabric so that the threads can enter the looper to make a stitch. A bent needle may enter too far away from the looper or can't even enter to make a stitch.

✂ Especially with the large amount of dust and fluff a serger creates, it is best to change your needles after every 4–6 hours of sewing.

✂ Needles too small cause imperfect stitches, as the thread cannot stay in the groove to form the loop picked up by the looper.

✂ If your serger has two needles, you have the option of changing the stitch width using one or two needles. Threading only the right needle gives a more narrow width.

Using the needle inserter.

Standard serger foot

The standard serger foot is used with most serging construction and finishing edges. It will be the foot most often used. The bottom of the foot is flat to keep fabric layers consistently in contact with the feed dogs.

On some serger models, the line on the far right of the foot shows the knife line when cutting width is set to 6mm (the most common width). The left outermost lines measure the distance from the cutting line.

On other models, the raised markings on the front of the foot indicate the position of the needles. They are helpful when inserting needles, as they match the openings in the needle bar, or when stitching over a previously stitched seam or drawn line.

Tape guide

Some models of the standard serger feet have an adjustable tape guide. There is an adjustable guide on top of the front of the standard serger foot that is useful when stitching twill tape or elastic, or applying elastic to lingerie. It will accommodate ribbons, tapes and elastic up to ¼" (6mm) in width.

Earn your stripes

Use striped fabric to become familiar with exactly where the knife blades are and how they work. Place the fabric so that the cutting blade cuts exactly on the line between the striped colors. Take a good look at where the stitching line falls as you serge.

Serger foot

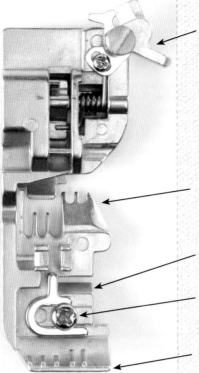

adjusts the pressure for seams on swimwear or other similar fabrics

lines up the needles for insertion

tape guide

The fixing screw loosens and adjusts the tape guide for width of tape.

Needle positions and/or cutting lines will be on the front.

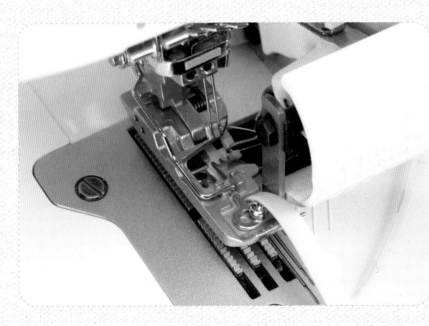

Using the tape guide

Loosen the fixing screw with a small screwdriver and slide the tape guide all the way to the left. Tighten the screw. Slip the twill tape or ribbon into the slot on the presser foot. Lower the presser foot and needles into the twill tape or ribbon. Loosen the fixing screw again and adjust the tape guide until the tape or ribbon fits snugly. Then retighten.

Specialty feet

Specialty feet are available to make some tasks easier. Some, but not all, might come with the serger, while others can be purchased separately. See what specialty feet came with your machine and begin accumulating others as necessary. Check your manual for the feet available for your serger. Not all the following feet are available on all sergers, and some may perform the same function but might be given a different name by the manufacturer.

Some commonly used feet are the gathering foot, blindstitch foot, beading foot, cover stitch foot, piping foot, the elasticator, and the multipurpose foot. As with learning any new skill, using any of the specialty feet also takes some practice.

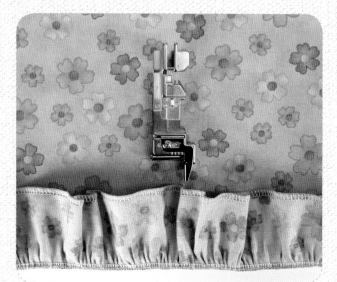

Gathering foot

The gathering foot is designed to gather fabric and also has the ability to gather and sew onto a second fabric at the same time. The foot is designed with a spring-loaded gathering flap on the underside of the foot. This flap separates the two fabrics, and when the foot is lowered, keeps the lower fabric firmly in place. Use a 2- or 3-thread overlock stitch.

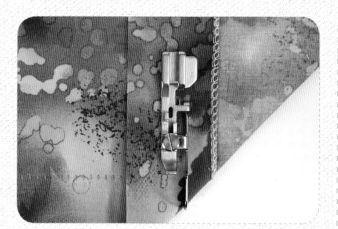

Blindstitch foot

The blindstitch foot is used to create a blind hem. It has one long side edge to guide the fabric fold. An adjustable blade guide keeps the folded fabric in line while the hem is stitched. Most of the blindstitch feet are intended to be used with the right needle only. This foot is especially suitable for medium to heavyweight knits and wovens. Use a 2- or 3-thread overlock stitch.

Line it up with the blade guide

When using the blindstitch foot, line up your fabric fold with the adjustable blade guide, not the fabric edge.

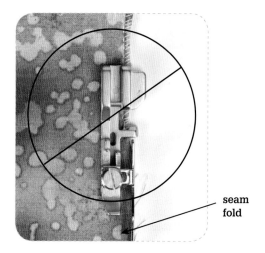

seam fold

Beading foot
The beading foot has a top groove for strings of beads, pearls and sequins. It allows for stitching size 4mm cords and strands of beads, sequins and pearls, as the foot guides the strand in a deep upper groove. Use a 3-thread overlock or flatlock stitch.

Cover stitch foot
This is used for cover stitch hemming, seaming, binding, inserting elastic, and adding zippers. The bottom of the foot is flat and has two or three needle slots, depending on the number of needles on your serger model. The "floating toes" compensate for uneven fabric layers and also help maintain perfect alignment of the stitching line. When using this foot, the knife guard is replaced with an extension plate.

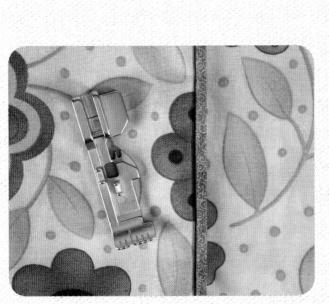

To make a piped zipper
Create piping and stitch to zipper tape. Place right side of fabric to zipper right side. Serge together.

Piping foot
The piping foot, used to create and attach piping, is designed with a groove underneath the foot to securely hold cord while stitching.

Multipurpose foot

Instead of a separate piping and beading foot, some manufacturers have a multipurpose foot. The foot is designed for a variety of serging tasks. It has a deep upper channel on the right side of the foot for stitching strands of beads, sequins and pearls. It also has a tunnel under the foot to allow making and attaching piping. A separate guide attaches to the serger to keep cord and piping fabrics lined up ahead of the stitching and to prevent tangling.

Elasticator

The elasticator foot stretches elastic while it's being serged. A hinged roller at the front of the foot stretches the elastic and also holds it in place under the foot. Adjust the degree of elastic stretch using a pressure screw located on the top of the foot. The greater the pressure, the more gathered the results will be. This foot is perfect for sewing swimwear, lingerie and sportswear. Use elastic that is 5mm to 12mm wide, and a 4-thread overlock stitch.

One-step elastic and fabric sewing

Use the elasticator foot to sew picot-edged elastic and fabric in one step. First, set your serger for a 2-, 3- or 4-thread overlock stitch. Place the elastic through the roller and adjust the screw to the elastic's width. Lay the elastic on the edge of the fabric, right sides together and fabric extending slightly beyond the elastic. Serge while guiding the elastic and fabric so only the fabric edge is trimmed.

Serger thread

A serger definitely uses much more thread than a conventional sewing machine. You will find thread on cones with as much as 10,000 yards (9,144m) and compact tubes having 1,000 yards (914m). Sounds like quite a bit of thread; however, for each yard (.9m) of stitching, you will use about 6 to 10 yards (5m to 9m) of thread. More thread will be used in the loopers than in the needles. Remember this when buying thread for a project, and grab those larger cones for the loopers.

You can serge with 100-percent cotton or synthetic thread, and cotton and synthetic blends. You can also use specialty threads with your serger, such as woolly nylon, pearl cotton, monofilament, and even yarn.

Q: Can you use any cone thread with a serger?
    –Cheryl Parker, Aurora, Illinois

Although any type of thread can be used in the serger, always choose the best quality thread you can find. A serger works at a high rate of speed—up to about 1,700 stitches per minute—and creates a lot more stress on the thread than a conventional sewing machine. Toss out poor-quality threads—those with uneven spots and fuzzy fibers along the strand—and only buy thread that will hold up to the speed of the serger.

Regular serger thread is a lighter-weight thread than other sewing thread. A lightweight thread works best on a serger, as there is more thread on the cone and the thinner thread reduces bulk. It is cross-wound onto cones or tubes for easy and even feeding. Serger thread can be the most economical, as there can be 2,000 to 10,000 yards (1,829m to 9,144m) per cone.

There are actually three forms of thread that can be used on a serger: (1) parallel-wound spool, (2) cross-wound spool, and (3) a cone. Whatever type you use, always keep in mind that more thread is used on the loopers than in the needles.

✄ **Parallel-wound** thread has been used for years on the conventional sewing machine and can still be used on the serger. The thread feeds from the side of the spool. As the serger goes at such a high rate of speed, it is best to use a spool cap.

✄ **Cross-wound** thread appears as a diamond pattern on the spool. It is very serger-friendly, as it feeds off the top of the spool.

✄ **Cone thread** is cross-wound also, feeding off the top. When using cone thread, use a cone holder to prevent the cone from shaking and rattling while stitching.

Thread weight affects tension. Heavy thread takes up more room in the tension control, so adjustment is necessary. Loosen to balance the tension, and choose a longer stitch length. Adjust accordingly to ensure the thread moves smoothly and evenly through all the guides and loopers. Adjustments can be made while serging, so always give the thread and fabric a good test run.

Some threads can improve certain serger stitches. For example, since its stretchy quality provides more coverage, using woolly stretch nylon for a rolled hem stitch will give you fewer "pokies"—small threads that poke from a serger-finished edge. See page 45 for a helpful guide on which threads are best, depending on the stitch you want to use.

Blendable color threads

It is not always necessary to use a thread color that perfectly matches the fabric, unless the finished stitching will be seen from both sides. You can even blend several shades into one seam. To save economically and also cut down on threading time, you might choose "blendable" threads. They are colors that go with almost everything. On light fabrics, they are ivory, creams, khaki and light browns. Gray works on dark fabrics. Other nice blendables to choose are light blue and light mauve. Thread shades of red, yellow and blue do not blend with many fabric colors. If you only have one spool of matching thread, and must have a good match for the stitch, use it in the needle at the seamline and other blendables elsewhere.

When choosing colors of thread, keep the following in mind:

✄ When sewing on a lightweight, sheer fabric or when you will see both sides, you may want all the threads to match.
✄ During seam construction, the needle thread shows when the seam is slightly pulled apart. If using two needles, only the left needle thread is visible.
✄ When serging with the right side up on hems, you will mostly see the upper looper thread.

Troubleshooting

The best way to learn what each thread does is to thread your serger with different colors in each thread path. This allows you to see which thread shows on the stitching, and which goes to each needle and each looper, and it is then easier to identify which thread is causing the problem. Remember to make note of this information and keep it handy.

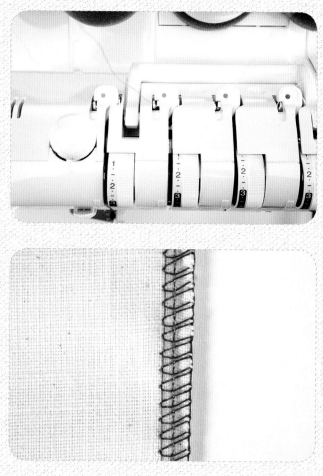

Watch for buildup

Cotton thread tends to create more lint buildup, so clean the tension disks and around the loopers regularly.

Using the Serger

Don't let your serger intimidate you. Learn the basics, take notes, and practice. Before long, you will be tackling challenging projects. What stitches are available for your specific serger? Open the manual and begin with the first stitch. Stitch some samples. Change threads. Test different types and weights of fabric. Jot down tension changes or stitch length and width adjustments in your manual or serger journal. Tape a sample of each on the page. With practice, you will begin to see the differences in each stitch.

Take the time to learn each part of your serger, especially what is inside the looper cover. Open this cover to have access to the lower knife, the upper looper release lever, the upper and lower looper, the roll hem lever, cutting width adjusting dial, lower knife setscrew, lower looper auto threader, and threading diagram. Check your manual and serger, as each model is different.

Start and end with a thread tail

Making a thread tail with a serger is different than with a sewing machine, as you begin stitching without fabric under the presser foot to create one using a serger. Then "stitch off" when you come to the end of your seam, serging at least 4" (10cm) beyond the fabric edge. The only exception is the cover stitch, when it is generally best to begin stitching on the fabric.

The thread tail created will keep threads from unraveling on the piece just serged, and the next piece will have an ample amount of thread when beginning—again, so threads don't unravel.

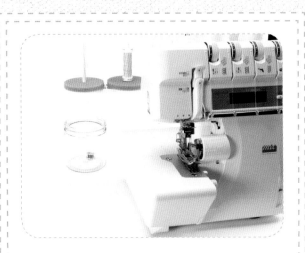

Decorative thread tip

When using small amounts of decorative thread, wind it on the bobbins from a sewing machine. Then place the bobbins on the spool pins to thread the needles, as they use lesser amounts of thread. If the bobbin will not fit onto the spool pins, place it in a small jar behind the serger. The bobbin may bounce around, but a free flow of thread will pass through the serger.

Threading

Panic attack! Time to thread your machine. Where do you even start? Threading a serger is similar to threading a sewing machine, in that all the guides and tension slots must be threaded properly. A serger can be more intimidating, as there can be one to two needles and several loopers to thread, instead of the one needle and single spool of thread on a sewing machine.

Several steps will ensure your serger is almost always threaded correctly:

1. Make sure the support rods are fully extended to give proper stitching.

2. Raise the needles by turning the handwheel in the normal sewing direction until they are fully raised.

3. Raise the presser foot so the tension is released.

4. Thread the serger carefully following the thread guide on your machine, and most importantly, be sure the thread is inserted properly in the tension slots.

5. Pull a sufficient amount of thread under the presser foot.

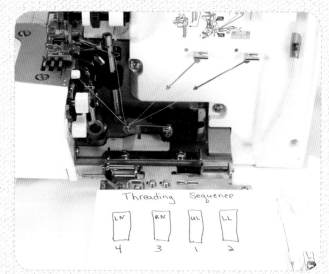

Threading sequence

There are not too many "musts" when using a serger, but the sequence of threading is very important. The right threading sequence is often not thought of, but is critical to keeping threads from tangling, fraying and breaking. You might want to make a small note of this sequence (check your manual first to make sure it's not different for your serger) and keep it beside your machine:

- ✂ Upper looper (UL)
- ✂ Lower looper (LL)
- ✂ Right-hand needle (RN)
- ✂ Left-hand needle (LN)

You are continually making adjustments on a serger when changing threads, fabric types and weights, and stitches. When threading the serger for a 2-thread overlock, rolled hem stitch or cover stitch, you will make additional adjustments, besides just changing the thread colors. The 2-thread overlock requires an upper looper converter, and for a rolled hem, the stitch tongue in the stitch plate must be disengaged. The cover stitch requires disengaging the upper looper, raising the upper knife, and exchanging the knife guard in the looper cover with a cover stitch extension plate. Check your manual thoroughly for specific adjustments you may need to make before serging with certain stitches.

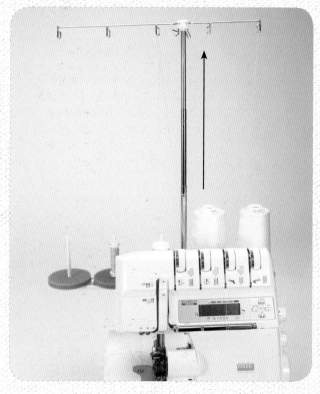

Support rods fully extended.

A fast method of changing threads

When changing threads, there is a faster method than pulling the thread out from all of the guides, loopers and needles. Remember to always rethread in the same sequence as shown on page 32. **NOTE:** This tie-on method won't work if changing to a heavyweight thread, as the knot may be too large to enter the eyes of the loopers.

1. Cut the thread right in front of the needles. Run the machine until you have about 6" (15cm) of thread tail. The machine will not form a chain, as the needles are not threaded.

2. Loosen the upper and lower looper tension.

3. Raise the presser foot to release the tension of the needle threads.

4. Cut the thread right above the spool.
Remove the thread and put on the new thread spool.

5. Tie the two ends together, and cut off excess threads to about 1" (3cm).

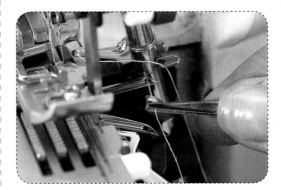

6. Run the serger, which will pull the threads through the guides and loopers.

You could also just pull one thread at a time.

7. When pulling the needle threads and you see the new thread close to the needle, stop. Cut the old thread, remove from the needle eye, and rethread with the new thread color. Never try to run the knot through the needle eye, as it will bend or break.

Make threading easier

Make threading easier by using the tweezers and threaders. It helps to have the tweezers and threaders pointing in the same direction toward the eye.

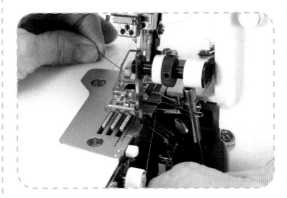

Threading heavyweight thread in the loopers can be made easy. Thread and follow the normal thread path, but stop before inserting heavy thread through the looper eye. Form a loop with all-purpose thread, and thread this through the looper eye. Place the heavy thread inside the loop and pull it through the eye.

Stitch length

The stitch length is the distance between between each stitch, where the needle enters the fabric. It is adjusted with a dial on the side or top of the serger. The stitch length has an infinite variable setting from 1–4mm on most machines. Most overlock stitching is done with a basic 2.5–3mm setting. Increasing the stitch length leaves more "space" between stitches. Decreasing (shortening) the stitch length gives more thread coverage.

When sewing heavier fabric, you may need to increase the stitch length. Threads can also have an effect on which stitch length is used. When using a very fine thread, you may need a shorter stitch length. When using decorative threads, the stitch length will be determined by the thickness of the thread, as well as the weight of the fabric.

A stitch length that is too long may pucker lightweight fabrics and may also show on the right side. Too short a stitch length will be weak, and some edges may stretch out of shape. Stitch length also affects the tension. Shorten the stitch to loosen the looper tension; lengthen to tighten the looper tension.

Stitch width

The cutting width is the stitch width on a serger—how far the cut edge of the fabric is from the needle. The width is usually controlled by a cutting width adjustment dial with numbers ranging from 1 to 5, corresponding to millimeters in size. Stitch length is also determined by which needle is used. A more narrow width can be created by using only the right needle.

Each number represents a different cutting width, with 1 being the smallest, and may differ among serger brands and models. The width is measured from the left needle if you have two needles, or the only needle if your serger has only one. If your serger has two needles, you can reduce the width even more by using only the right needle (closest to the cutting blade) and removing the left one.

The stitch width chosen is based mostly on the fabric type. However, the weight of the fabric is a critical consideration. Use a narrow stitch width for lightweight fabrics, medium stitch width for medium weight, and a wide stitch width for heavyweight fabrics. If the stitch width is too narrow, seams may not lay flat, or be strong enough for heavyweight fabrics. Some seams may even begin to unravel. A stitch width too

adjustment dial no. 4 stitch width

adjustment dial no. 1 stitch width

wide may cause puckering on sheer fabrics. Basic serger construction uses a stitch width of 6mm. Most of the projects in this book indicate a basic stitch width.

The most common widths available on serger models are:

- ✄ 5mm (³⁄₁₆")
- ✄ 6mm (¼")
- ✄ 7mm (⁹⁄₃₂")
- ✄ 8mm (⁵⁄₁₆")
- ✄ 9mm (¹¹⁄₃₂")

Stitch width affects the looper tensions. Narrow the stitch to loosen looper tension; widen the stitch to tighten looper tension.

Tension

Tension on a serger works the same as on a sewing machine. When the presser foot is raised, the tension is released. The serger has a tension area for each needle and each looper, whereas the sewing machine has tension for only the needle and the bobbin.

Tension is maintained through specific tension guides for each spool of thread used and each needle. Each spool of thread and needle corresponds to specific tension areas. Going from left to right at the top of your serger, the tension guides are:

- ✂ Left needle tension
- ✂ Right needle tension
- ✂ Upper looper tension
- ✂ Lower looper tension

It can be helpful to mark each one. You can then see at a glance not only which tension controls what area, but also which threads correspond to the serger part. If you are wanting to put decorative thread in one of the loopers, you will quickly know where to place the thread.

Each tension guide is controlled with a dial or lever. It may be marked with numbers, or a plus and minus sign. Most serger models work the same as a conventional sewing machine—the higher the number, the looser the tension. Check your manual to determine which direction to turn the dial (or lever) to increase or decrease the tension.

Not readily seen are tension disks that apply internal pressure on the complete tension mechanism. When you adjust the tension, you are actually adjusting the tension disks to place more or less pressure on the thread.

Tension plays a key role in forming the various stitches. For example, on my machine, the tension of the upper and lower loopers and the needle for a 3-thread overlock is 4.0. When changing to a 2-thread overlock, I set the lower looper to 6.0 and the needle to 2.0–3.0. This maintains a balanced serger stitch. Check your manual for a stitch formation guide and suggested tensions.

left needle tension   right needle tension   upper looper tension   lower looper tension

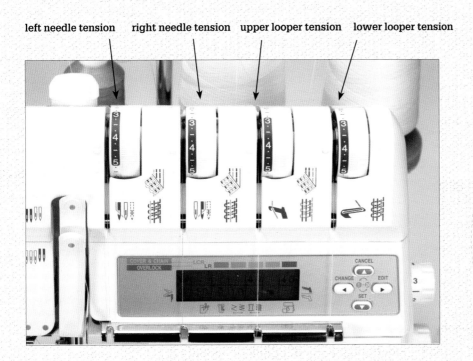

Threads loopy?

Loopy threads indicate too loose of tension. If you can't determine which looper or needle is causing the problem, begin with the upper looper. Increase the tension and test. Continue with the lower looper and the needles if necessary.

Differential feed adjustment

Machines with differential feed have two sets of feed dogs. The front ones move the fabric toward the needle, while the back ones move the fabric after the stitches are made. Differential feed eliminates puckers and wavy edges, and can also be used for gathering.

Check your manual when adjusting the differential feed, as most machines have a numbered dial. The normal setting may be indicated with an N. When lightweight or stretchy fabric begins to pucker, try moving the dial to a smaller number.

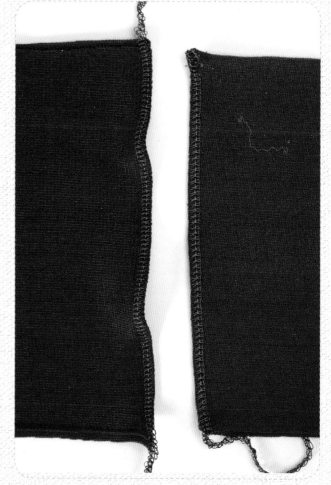

For gathering

Use differential feed to gather. Adjust for gathering by moving to a larger number. Serge near the edge, trimming slightly. The serger gathers the fabric automatically.

Pressure regulator

The pressure regulator adjusts the pressure of the presser foot and ultimately, the movement of the fabric. Most are usually a screw on the top of the machine. Turn clockwise to increase pressure and counterclockwise to decrease pressure. Heavy fabrics benefit from an increased pressure to prevent skipped stitches.

Clearing the fingers

When serging, stitches are formed around one or two stitch fingers located on the needle plate or the presser foot. Stitches are always left chained around the stitch fingers at the end of each seam.

There are times when it is necessary to clear (remove) stitches from the needle plate or the presser foot. This is referred to as "clearing the fingers." You might clear the fingers when you turn outside corners or when changing the needle plate. To clear the fingers, lift the presser foot and raise the needles. Pull about a ½" (12mm) slack in each needle thread right above the needles. Pull on the thread tail to release the stitches from the stitch fingers.

Using a rolled hem lever to clear

If your machine has a rolled hem lever, you may be able to use it to clear the stitch fingers. Pull it toward you to clear, and push back toward the machine when you begin stitching again. Check your manual for specific instructions.

Watch and listen as Charlene threads her serger, explaining the ins and outs of the threading process, at http://www.marthapullen.com/simply-serging.html.

Securing thread tails

When coming to the end of the seam using a serger, you want to continue stitching beyond the fabric's edge until you have a thread tail long enough to cut or to secure (see photo on page 31). This is referred to as stitching off or chaining off.

Securing thread tails works the same as a reverse stitch in sewing; it locks the stitches in place. If you are going to be serging over one seam with another seam, you don't need to secure the thread tail. Just cut if off at least several inches (or centimeters) beyond the fabric edge. If you are not serging over the seam, you need to secure the thread tail to *finish* the seam. There are several ways to accomplish this.

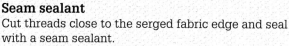

Seam sealant
Cut threads close to the serged fabric edge and seal with a seam sealant.

Tuck into seam
Tuck the thread tail back into the stitches using a tapestry needle or loop turner. Thread the needle with the threads and weave under the overlocked stitches about 2" (5cm). Cut off any remaining threads.

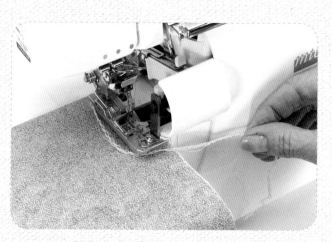

At the beginning of the seam, serge over thread tails to secure
Serge a thread chain about 3" to 4" (8cm to 10cm) long. Raise the presser foot, and gently pull the thread tail to the front and toward the serger, so it lies on the top of the seam being stitched. Lower the foot, serge over the thread tail, and continue sewing.

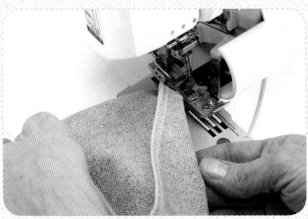

Make one stitch past end of seam, then stop

Raise the presser foot and the needle, and clear the
stitch fingers. Turn the fabric over, and align the edge
of the seam with the edge of the knives. Lower the
presser foot and stitch over the previous seam about 1"
to 1½" (3cm to 4cm) *without* cutting the serged edge.
Angle the stitch off the edge, leaving a thread tail. Cut
the thread close to the seam edge.

knife window

Serging curves (and circles)

Sergers love gentle curves. There are two
methods of starting to serge a curve: (1) angle the
stitches onto and off the fabric, or (2) cut a "knife"
window in the fabric.

For the first option, slowly serge around the
curve while guiding the fabric. Periodically, lift the
presser foot and adjust the fabric. Lower the foot
and continue. When you return to the beginning
stitches, stop and lift the presser foot. Shift the
fabric so it is behind the needle, and stitch off the
edge. This prevents a buildup of stitches.

If you use the knife window technique, cut a
rectangle about 1" (3cm) in depth and 2" (5cm)
long at the fabric edge. Place the presser foot so
that the right needle falls in the front left corner of
the knife window. Begin serging around the circle,
and when you return to the knife window, serge
over the first stitches and angle off.

Serging corners

Q: What is the best way to serge corners?
  –Gloria Wright, Myra, Kentucky

Q: What is the best way to get a good-looking inside corner when serging?
  –Joyce Shellito, Columbia Heights, Minnesota

Due to the size and shape of a serger's presser foot, fabric cannot be turned too quickly. Fabric cannot be sharply pivoted on corners because the threads are chained around the stitch fingers. On inside corners, the knives have trimmed the fabric to the corner before the needle actually stitches it. Despite this, several techniques will make you the master of your serger.

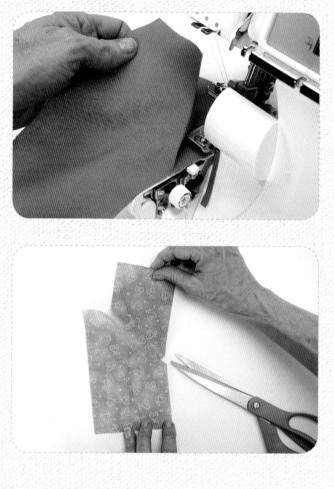

Outside corner

There are several methods to stitch an outside corner; however, the easiest is to serge each side separately. Serge one edge of the fabric, stitching off the end of the corner. Begin serging again, going over the previously serged edge. Repeat for each side corner, going over the previous stitching. Secure remaining thread tails using any of the methods previously mentioned.

An alternative method is to trim the seams about 2" (5cm), or the distance between the needle and the cutting blade. This allows ease of pivoting. Serge to the corner, taking one stitch off the fabric. Raise the needle from the fabric, and clear the finger of stitches. Turn the fabric a quarter turn counterclockwise, then place the needle one stitch into the fabric. Gently tug on all the threads from behind the foot to remove any slack. Lower the foot and continue serging.

Inside corner

Stitch up to the inside corner, and fold the fabric to the left to straighten the edge. Stitch through the corner, keeping fabric in a straight line. If necessary, fold the fabric before placing under the serger.

An alternative to stitching inside corners is to cut a slit in the corner. Mark the seamlines for about 2" (5cm) on both sides of the corner. Clip into the corner about ⅛" (3mm) short of the marked lines. Serge the seam until the knife just comes to the corner, then stop with the needle down in the fabric. Raise the presser foot and straighten the corner carefully, then lower the foot and continue stitching.

Serged inside corner

For a successful slit

Try folding the fabric before placing it under the presser foot (see photo below). Serge slowly when reaching the corner, straightening the fabric as you serge.

Slit

For a slit, align the raw edge of the fabric with the serger knives. Serge, stopping when the knives reach the corner. Straighten the edges of the fabric to distribute fullness. Continue stitching, keeping the fabric in a straight line.

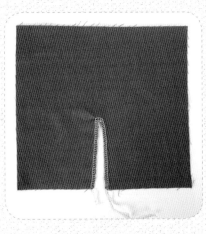

Serged slit

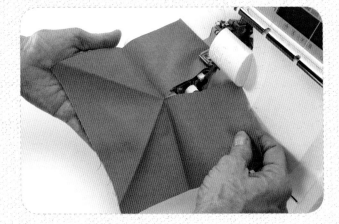

Eliminating bulk

To eliminate bulk when sewing corners with a regular sewing machine, we usually clip the corners. Not so with the serger! Try wrapping the corners to reduce bulk and to create nice, crisp corners. This creates a "wrapped" edge. This method works on nearly every corner seam, especially those which will be between layers of fabric, such as collars.

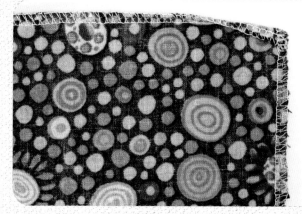

1. Place right sides together and serge one of the edges, corner to corner. Remove from the machine.

2. Press the seam flat and toward the body of the fabric.

3. Serge the opposite seam, enclosing the wrapped corner. Repeat for each side. Turn to right side and press.

Another way to eliminate bulk is to offset the seam allowance by pressing the seams in opposite directions.

Stabilized seams

There are times you will want to stabilize seams and prevent stretching, especially in garment construction, or possibly when working with vinyl. Other times, stitches tend to pull away from the edge, as with delicate fabrics such as lamés. Stabilizing the edge almost guarantees a perfect edge. As with any sewing, the type of fabric and the final effect you want will determine the type of stabilizer and which of these methods to use:

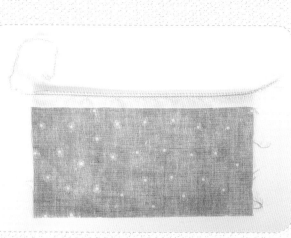

✄ Place water-soluble stabilizer either over or under the edge to be serged.
✄ Place a layer of Seams Great or Stitch Witchery tape under the edge to be serged.

Other items, such as tapes, ribbons, interfacing and tricot bias binding can be used for stabilizing, depending on the type of fabric.

✄ **Nonstretch:** Use twill tape, ribbon or seam tape.
✄ **Fusible:** Use a strip of fusible interfacing.
✄ **Slight stretch:** Use tricot bias binding where a slight stretch is necessary.

General troubleshooting

Q: Is there a best thread to pull or cut to remove the stitching faster?

–Joyce Shellito, Columbia Heights, Minnesota

Every once in a while we must rip out those stitches, no matter how experienced we may be. First, locate the thread for each needle stitch. The 2- and 3-thread overlock stitches will have only one needle thread. The needle threads will be the shortest in the chain. Smoothing out the loops in the thread tail will help. Hold the needle threads and push the tail chain stitches close to the end of the fabric.

Pull the needle threads until they can be removed. The fabric will tend to gather. If the seam is long, snipping the looper threads about every 12" (31cm) can help. Once the needle threads are removed, pull the looper threads to finish clearing the seam.

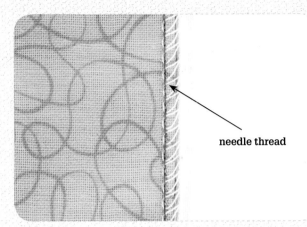

needle thread

Q: How do I work with the cover stitch when sewing in a circle?

–Monica Helton, Oxford, Ohio

When starting and stopping the cover stitch at a raw edge, nothing additional needs to be done. Secure threads as you normally would for any serging. However, if the cover stitch will be started and ended at the same place, as in a circle, then additional steps are necessary.

1. Begin stitching the cover stitch. Stop after about 3" (8cm). Snip the excess threads on top.
2. Continue serging until you reach the initial stitches. Slowly stitch several stitches over the initial ones.
3. Pull about 2" (5cm) of thread above the needles. Carefully pull the fabric toward the back and remove.

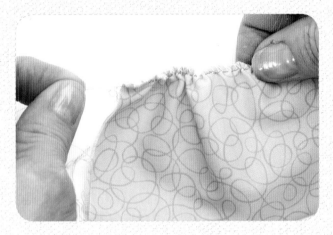

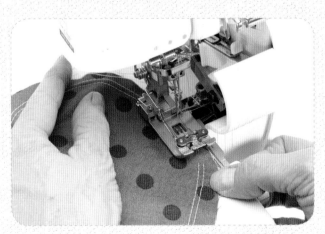

Q: What do I do when the fabric and/or threads jam?

–*Monica Helton, Oxford, Ohio*

If your needles are stuck in the "up" position when it jams, cut the needle threads and remove the presser foot. Gently tug on the fabric, pulling toward the back of the machine. If it just won't budge, cut the looper threads near the fabric and pull the fabric from the machine. Rethread and replace the presser foot.

If your needles are stuck in the fabric and in a "down" position, loosen the set screws of the needles and raise the needle bar. You will see the needles stuck in the fabric. Remove the presser foot and cut the needle and the looper threads close to the fabric. Gently pull the needles from the fabric, and pull the fabric toward the back of the serger to remove it. Insert new needles, rethread, and replace the presser foot.

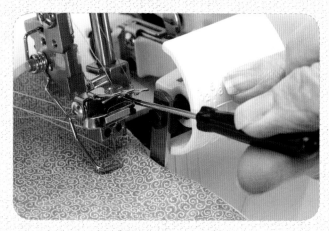

Check your stitch length

Fabric jams may occur if the stitch length is too short. The fabric won't feed properly through the serger, and stitches build up on the stitch fingers.

Watch and listen as Charlene shows you a quick trick for changing serger threads at http://www.marthapullen.com/simply-serging.html.

Threading guide

Not sure which threads to put in the needle and which to put in the loopers? Or, which threads work best for each serger stitch? Then keep this chart handy.

Application	Thread	Where to thread
overlock and cover stitch	all-purpose thread, polyester	needles and looper
rolled hems or soft seams in knits	woolly stretch nylon	loopers only
seams in most fabrics	all-purpose thread, polyester	needles and loopers
finishing/neatening edges	continuous filament, polyester	loopers only
rolled hems, cover stitch, and neatening edges	embroidery, darning or decorative threads	loopers only; very fine, lightweight thread can be used in needles also
decorative, rolled hems, flatwork	heavier rayon threads	loopers only
decorative uses	super-fine metallics	needles and loopers
decorative, rolled hems, flatwork	yarns	loopers only
secure edges, hems and seams	fusible thread	lower looper only
decorative, rolled hems, flatwork	ribbon and ribbon floss	loopers only

PART 2

THE PROJECTS

Most of these projects are completed using the serger only. Several of them involve your trusty sewing machine. These projects give you more knowledge of what can be done, and not done, on a serger. Start thinking "serger sewing" and you may try a decorative edging with the serger instead of the sewing machine topstitch, or an alternative to adding pockets. Give it a try, and see what *you* come up with!

Helpful Hints Before You Start

Seam allowance

All projects are stitched with a ⅝" (16mm) seam unless noted otherwise.

Sizing

Each pattern can be adjusted to fit what you really need. One size doesn't always fit all. When adapting any project to make smaller or larger, always be sure to add a ⅝" (16mm) seam allowance. Remember, the fabric will be cut as you serge.

Move smoothly

Serge at a nice, even pace. Remember to serge at least a 4" to 6" (10cm to 15cm) thread tail at the beginning and end of each seam. If the seam will be serged over, trim the threads close to the fabric.

Binding

Adding binding to your project is always an option. There are several methods that can be used; try each one to find your favorite:

✂ **Use your sewing machine to add binding**, following your favorite method.

✂ **Use the serger's overlock stitch.** Enclose the raw edge with binding and overcast in place. Keep the binding edge close to the knife, but do *not* cut into the binding while serging. A narrow binding works best for this method. Match the thread and binding color, unless you want a nice contrast.

✂ **Use the serger's cover stitch.** Set the serger for the cover stitch according to your manual. Wrap bias binding around the edge, and secure in place. Place the fabric under the needles, with the folded edge of the binding even with the inside of the "floating toe" of the cover stitch foot. Stitch the binding edge, then secure and trim excess threads.

Binding overcast with the serger.

Binding added using the serger's cover stitch feature.

Gathering

When gathering fabric, cut the fabric strip two and a half times the finished length. Whether gathering with the standard serger foot or using the gathering foot, adjust the serger for a gathering stitch. When using the standard serger foot, control gathers by raising the needle tension to the highest number.

The gathering foot (see page 26) offers more control than the standard serger foot and gathers a wider range of fabrics. To achieve maximum fullness, increase the differential setting (see page 36), use two needles instead of one (if possible), increase the stitch length to 4mm, and increase the foot pressure to the highest setting.

You can also use the gathering foot to gather one piece while simultaneously sewing it to a second piece of fabric. Place the piece to be gathered right side *up* under the foot (place against the feed dogs). Place the second fabric right side *down* between the slots on the gathering foot. Set the serger accordingly and begin stitching.

When gathering, place the first fabric right side up under the gathering foot, and the second fabric right side down.

Serger tip
If gathering multiple layers of fabric, baste them together first and treat as one fabric.

Making and turning a tube

Making and turning a tube to create a waistband or straps is quick and easy using the serger—even for tubes as thin as spaghetti straps.

1 Set the serger for a 3-thread overlock stitch. Serge a long strip of thread that is at least 6" (15cm) longer than the finished tube. *Don't* cut from the serger.

2 Fold the fabric strip in half, with right sides together. Then, fold back the serged strip of thread and place inside the folded fabric, near the fold. Serge the raw edges, making sure not to catch the serged strip of thread in the stitches. Stitch off at least 4" (10cm).

3 Pull on the serged thread, turning the fabric right sides out.

Serger tip
The three-thread overlock stitch uses less thread, so it is perfect for creating skinnier straps. A four-thread overlock stitch can be successfully used if the strap is much wider.

No serging over pins

When sewing with a sewing machine, we use pins all the time. In the excitement of serging a new project, it can be easy to forget about pin placement. Although mentioned earlier, this is important enough to repeat: Never, ever serge over pins. Either remove them before they get near the knives, or place them a distance from the raw edge. There are nice alternatives to pins, as mentioned earlier. For smaller pieces, try using a glue stick to hold pieces together while serging.

Instead of pinning, use a glue stick or painter's tape to keep pieces together as you serge.

Preventing ragged edges or "pokies" on rolled hems

Test-sew a rolled edge hem on your fabric. Some fabrics, such as metallic, lightweight woven or heavy stiff fabrics, don't fold under as nicely as others while serging. Instead, they cause an unattractive ragged edge.

There are various methods to eliminate those jagged edges. One is to use woolly stretch nylon thread (see page 29), since it has better coverage than other threads because of its stretch. Another method is use a strip of water-soluble stabilizer; place it on the raw edge and serge as usual, then rinse off the stabilizer when finished. Another method is to use a strip of tricot bias binding or hem facing. Place it on the upper side of the edge to be hemmed; serge, catching the binding in the stitching. Trim the excess tricot bias binding close to the rolled hem stitches.

If all else fails and pokies persist, apply sealant to the serged edges.

"Pokies" can jut out from an otherwise nicely rolled hem.

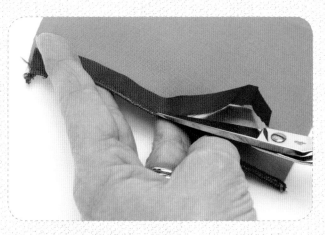

Trim excess tricot bias binding close to the rolled hem edge. Here, the binding is shown in a different color so the cutting can be seen better.

Guiding and cutting fabric

Remember that the serger is designed so the knives cut the fabric right before stitching. This leaves little room for error. Trimming mistakes are not easy to remedy. Practice with your serger before sewing and become very familiar with exactly where the knife blades are and where they are going to cut. Whatever the seam allowance given, stitch so that the left needle is that measurement from the edge of the fabric. For example, if there is a 5/8" (16mm) seam allowance, make sure the left needle is 5/8" (16mm) from the edge of the fabric.

For a 5/8" (16mm) seam allowance, the left needle needs to be 5/8" (16mm) from the edge of the fabric.

Adding Velcro

Velcro should be sewn on with your sewing machine, not the serger. The only alternative would be to use the chain stitch, which may not be as durable as you want. Whether you use a sewing machine or try the serger is your preference.

Rounding corners

At times, the instructions will have you "round the corners" of the fabric before serging. Trace using a paper plate to help with this.

Trace with a paper plate to round off your corners.

Avoid flying needles!

Let the serger do the work. Never push the fabric through the serger, and avoid excessive pulling on the fabric from behind the needle.

Adapt patterns

Although a serger is a complementary addition to your sewing room, many items can be constructed on the serger alone with minimal adaptation from a sewing machine pattern. Begin adapting patterns that have few seams. Review your pattern to determine what changes you might make in the order of construction to take advantage of your serger. For example, serge a sleeve into the body of the blouse before serging the sleeve into a tube. Soon you will find ways to use your serger throughout the sewing process.

Watch and listen as Charlene shows you what a serger looks like in action at http://www.marthapullen.com/simply-serging.html.

Memo Pad and Portfolio Cover

Turn your ordinary 5" × 8" (13cm × 20cm) memo pad into something special with a few layering techniques and your serger. Add fabric-covered elastic to keep it closed when tucked into a purse or briefcase. Rather not enclose the elastic in fabric? Simply skip the step for enclosing elastic and begin with the steps for assembling using the elastic. Instructions are also given for an 8½" × 11" (22cm × 28cm) portfolio cover.

Materials

(for memo)

* Cover fabric: 18" × 7" (46cm × 18cm)
* Lining fabric: 17" × 7" (43cm × 18cm)
* Pockets, cut 2: 17½" × 7" (44cm × 18cm)
* Pencil holders: 4" (10cm) piece of grosgrain ribbon (optional—tube method to make tabs)
* Elastic: 1" × 8" (25mm × 20cm)
* Elastic casing: 3" × 7½" (8cm × 19cm)

(for portfolio)

* Cover fabric: 25" × 10½" (64cm × 27cm)
* Lining fabric: 24½" × 10½" (62cm × 27cm)
* Pockets, cut 2: 25" × 10½" (64cm × 27cm)
* Pencil holders: 4" (10cm) piece of grosgrain ribbon (optional—tube method to make tabs)
* Elastic: 1" × 12" (25mm × 30cm)
* Elastic casing: 3" × 10½" (8cm × 27cm)

Serger settings

* 3 or 4 thread overlock
* **Stitch length:** 2.5 to 3mm
* **Stitch width:** 6mm
* **Cutting blade:** ON
* **Foot:** Standard serger foot

Remember to...
Always thread with the presser foot in the raised position. This releases the tension and allows the thread to "seat" properly between the tension disks.

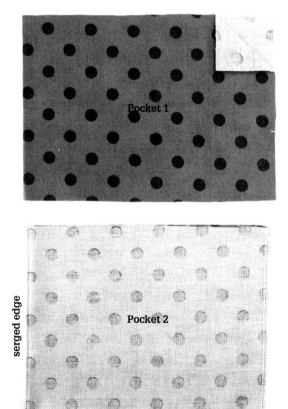

Pocket 1

serged edge

Pocket 2

1 Prepare the pockets first. Fold Pocket 1 wrong sides together and press. Set aside. Fold Pocket 2 right sides together and serge the short, raw edges together. Turn right sides out and press. Set aside.

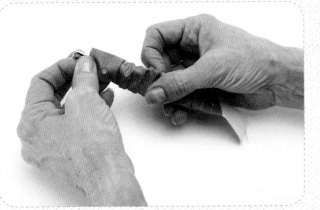

2 Prepare the casing as when making a tube (*see Making and turning a tube, page 50*). Slide elastic inside the casing, matching the ends of the elastic with the raw fabric edge. Tack in place if you wish. Gather the excess fabric toward the center. Set aside.

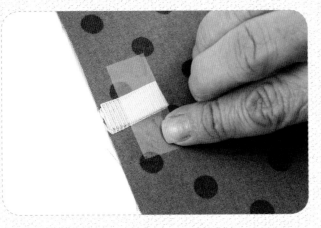

3 Fold each 2" (5cm) ribbon piece in half. Find the center of the memo cover fabric. Place one piece of ribbon on the center mark of both short ends, matching raw fabric edge and cut ribbon edge. Tape in place.

4 Place Pocket 1 along one short raw edge of the memo cover fabric, matching the raw edges, and serge. Trim excess threads.

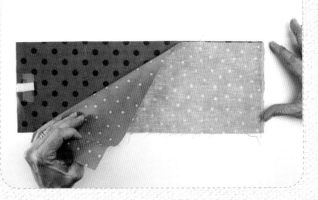

5 Place the memo cover fabric and lining right sides together, matching the raw edges of the opposite short edge. Serge. Trim excess threads. Open and press the seam.

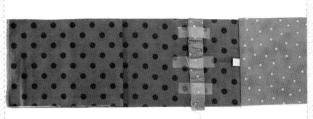

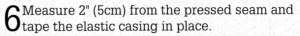

6 Measure 2" (5cm) from the pressed seam and tape the elastic casing in place.

7 Place Pocket 2 along the seam, on top of the elastic casing. Tuck the folded edge as close to the seam as possible.

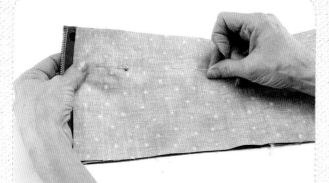

8 Fold the lining piece on top of the pocket pieces and the main cover fabric. Serge along both long edges.

9 Turn the memo cover right sides out and press.

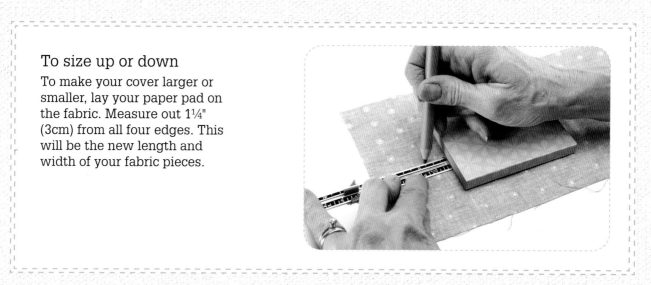

Customize it

All variations are up to you! Add a contrasting strip to the outside, or a patchwork strip. Embroider your name. Or, instead of having pencil tabs or the elastic casing, add long strips of lace to tie the memo cover closed.

To size up or down

To make your cover larger or smaller, lay your paper pad on the fabric. Measure out 1¼" (3cm) from all four edges. This will be the new length and width of your fabric pieces.

Rose Accessory

There may be more than a hundred species of roses, but this one will surely make a statement. With just a strip of fabric, quickly adorn a garment, or create an attachable accessory. Add to your purse, lapel or a headband. Embellish with beading for a classy look, or sequins for something more shimmery. Try this with a variety of silks, such as dupioni, chiffon or china silk. Have a fabric that doesn't ravel? Make your rose with a rolled hem instead of doubling the fabric.

Materials

* Rose fabric: 4" × 56" (10cm × 142cm) strip
* Pin back (comb back or hair clip for hair accessory)
* 4" (10cm) square of felt
* Optional: Leaf fabric in two 3" or 4" (8cm or 10cm) squares

Serger settings

(for gathering)

* 3 or 4 thread overlock
* **Stitch length:** 4mm
* **Stitch width:** 2.5 to 3mm
* **Cutting blade:** ON
* **Differential feed:** 1.5 to 2
* **Foot:** Standard serger foot (Optional: Gathering foot)

(for rolled hem, if desired)

* 2 or 3 thread rolled hem
* **Stitch length:** 1mm
* **Stitch width:** 5 to 6mm
* **Cutting blade:** ON
* **Differential feed:** Adjust as necessary
* **Foot:** Standard serger foot

If available, engage rolled hem lever

1 Fold the rose fabric in half lengthwise, with wrong sides together. Round off the top raw-edge corners.

2 Working with the raw edges, begin serging/gathering along one rounded edge (opposite the folded edge). Continue along the raw edges, and toward the opposite rounded edge. Secure and trim excess threads.

Gathering 101

✂ The trick to gathering with the standard serger foot is the needle settings. Set both right and left needles at the highest settings; for example, on my machine, that is 9. I set my differential feed between 1.5 and 2 (see page 36).

✂ Along with the serger settings, the amount of gather depends on the weight of the fabric. Lightweight fabrics gather much fuller than cottons, and the length of the strip may be shorter.

✂ In addition to fabric weight, cutting the fabric on the bias can also add to the gathering effect. Adjust the length of the strip according to the fabric. Sheer fabrics can be made with a smaller strip.

✂ To prevent your gathering stitches from ungathering, stitch a thread tail of at least 7" (18cm). Cut the thread chain, but don't pull on the fabric or all your work will be lost.

✂ On the other hand, if you find you have too much gather in your fabric, give a gentle pull on the edge of the fabric. Adjust the gathers evenly.

3 Begin folding the fabric in a circle to form the rose. Vary how tight you fold the rose to get the effect you want. While folding, hand-stitch raw edges to hold the gathers in place.

4 Glue the circle of felt to the back with a glue gun to cover the stitches.

Try a single layer
Instead of a double layer of fabric, try single layers. Stitch a rolled hem along one edge, and round the opposite corners. Gather the raw edge, and finish following the same steps. Try using knits for a nonraveling edge.

Add flair to the edges

Add beading, pearls or sequins to edges using the beading foot or the serger multipurpose foot. Stranded beads or pearls should not be larger than 3mm in diameter. If serging sequins, they should not be larger than 5mm and should overlap in the direction of the sewist so the strand feeds smoothly under the foot.

1. Place the beading (pearls or sequins) in the right side channel of the multipurpose foot, or the channel in the beading foot, and draw under to the back of the foot.

2. Serge a few stitches to secure.

3. Place fabric under the foot and serge in place. Secure threads.

If beading, pearls or sequins are going to be located in the seam, pull several off the strand before serging up to the seam.

5 Sew or glue on the pin back or hair clip.

Optional: Make leaves
Fold a leaf fabric square in half. Bring each corner to the middle, and press. Hand sew the leaves to the back.

(project shown completed by Megan McGuire)

Baby's Receiving Blanket

Surprise the mom-to-be with a receiving blanket
made just for her little one. Edge the blanket with a
lovely rolled hem of matching or contrasting color.
This blanket measures 34" × 52" (86cm × 132cm);
however, you can easily adjust the size if necessary.

(project shown completed by Megan McGuire)

Materials

* Blanket fabric: 1 yard (.9m)

Serger settings

* **2 or 3 thread rolled hem**
* **Stitch length:** 1mm
* **Stitch width:** 5 to 6mm
* **Cutting blade:** ON
* **Foot:** Standard serger foot

If available, engage rolled hem lever

Avoid pesky pokies

To avoid having "pokies" in any rolled hem (see page 51), use woolly stretch nylon thread. The thread is a soft, stretchy, untwisted nylon that spreads over the edge nicely. Place a net over the spool to avoid tangling and twisting.

Remember to...

Remove the left needle for a rolled hem. Also disengage the stitch finger. Your machine may have a lever to press. Loosen the upper tension so the threads are pulled underneath the stitch. It may also help to tighten the lower tension. Be sure to test on scrap fabric first!

1 Cut the fabric to 36" × 53" (92cm × 135cm). Set your serger for a rolled edge hem.

2 Round off each corner (see page 52) to make a gentle curve.

3 Serge around all four sides, going slowly around the curves. Secure and trim the excess threads.

Try a burp cloth

Make a matching burp cloth with prewashed flannel. Cut two pieces of fabric to measure 19" × 11" (48cm × 28cm). Place wrong sides together and serge around all sides. Trim any excess threads and secure.

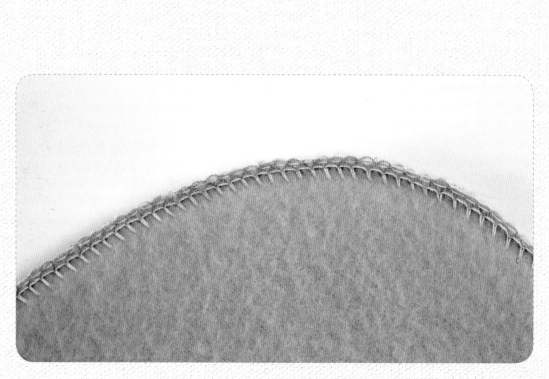

Blanket stitch hem

Make a receiving blanket from fleece and edge with a blanket stitch. This stitch resembles the overcasting stitch used on the edges of scarves, blankets and other bulky items.

Crumb-Catcher Baby Bib

A baby bib of sorts has been around for a long time, always with the intention of keeping a baby's clothes clean. With a little bit of fabric you can stitch up quite a few! Rolled hems and lovely soft curves are tasks the serger does quite well.

(project shown completed by Megan McGuire)

FOLD

Bib template
Enlarge 200%; shown at 50%.

Crumb-catcher template
Enlarge 200%;
shown at 50%.

Materials

* Bib fabric: 10" × 16" (25cm × 41cm)
* Crumb-catcher fabric: 3" × 10" (8cm × 25cm)
* 2" (5cm) Velcro piece
* Bib and crumb-catcher templates (page 64)

Serger settings

* 2 or 3 thread rolled hem
* **Stitch length:** 1mm
* **Stitch width:** 5 to 6mm
* **Cutting blade:** ON
* **Foot:** Standard serger foot

If available, engage rolled hem lever

1 Cut the main bib and crumb-catcher pieces from the fabric according to the templates.

2 Stitch a rolled hem edge at the top of the crumb-catcher piece.

5 Sew Velcro to the neck ties using your sewing machine.

3 Lay the crumb-catcher in place on the bib piece and pin to secure.

4 Starting at the back of the bib, serge a rolled edge hem all the way around, catching the crumb-catcher in the rolled hem.

Add a saying

A nice variation is to make the bib from oilcloth for easy wiping. Need a quick baby gift? Personalize the bib by embroidering the baby's name or a cute saying.

Placemats

Today's oilcloth is vinyl with a cotton backing fused on. There are also new laminated fabrics that are cotton with a slick top, like oilcloth, yet are lighter in weight and much easier to sew. These placemats are so simple to make that you will want a set for each season of the year. Add a pocket to hold a napkin and flatware. Use your sewing machine to add the pocket, or try the serger's cover stitch. Go a step further and make matching linen napkins.

Materials

(for one placemat)

※ Oilcloth fabric (for placemat): 13" × 19" (33cm × 48cm)

※ Oilcloth fabric (for pocket): 4" × 10" (10cm × 25cm)

Serger settings

※ 2 or 3 thread rolled hem

※ **Stitch length:** 1mm

※ **Stitch width:** 5 to 6mm

※ **Cutting blade:** ON

※ **Foot:** Standard serger foot

If available, engage rolled hem lever

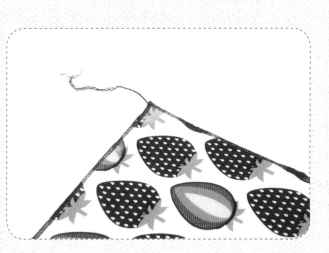

1 Begin serging the placemat. When reaching a corner, sew straight off the edge. Start serging at the same corner, serging over the previously serged edge.

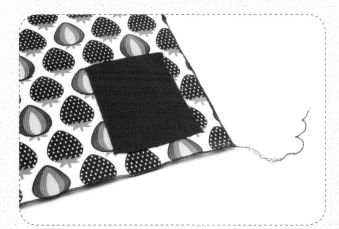

2 For the pocket, fold fabric in half with wrong sides together to make a 4" × 5" (10cm × 13cm) piece. Serge a rolled edge hem at the top and along the two side raw edges. Place the pocket 1" (3cm) from the right side and 1" (3cm) from the bottom. Using the sewing machine, stitch in place using a straight or narrow zigzag stitch; or, use your serger's cover stitch to sew the pocket on the placemat.

3 Stitch a rolled edge hem all around the placemat. Secure and cut off excess threads.

Napkins to match

Make a quick set of matching napkins. For each linen napkin, cut a 17" (43cm) square. Finish the edges with a rolled edge hem.

Rayon for a rolled edge

Rayon thread makes a beautiful rolled edge hem. Use in the upper looper only.

Cell Phone Purse

A major shopping trip to the sewing shop requires both hands free! Tuck your cell phone into this purse and your money in the pocket. You can easily make the cell phone purse with a pocket or without. Vary the size to suit your needs. Make the strap from cording or ribbon, and keep it long or shorten it as desired.

Materials

✳ Cover fabric: 7½" × 10" (19cm × 25cm)

✳ Lining: 7½" × 10" (19cm × 25cm)

✳ Pocket: 7½" × 10" (19cm × 25cm)

✳ 42" (107cm) ribbon

Serger settings

✳ 3 or 4 thread overlock

✳ **Stitch length:** 2.5 to 3mm

✳ **Stitch width:** 6 to 7mm

✳ **Cutting blade:** ON

✳ **Differential feed:** Adjust as necessary

✳ **Foot:** Standard serger foot

1 Fold the lining fabric in half crosswise. Finger press a crease. Lay right side up.

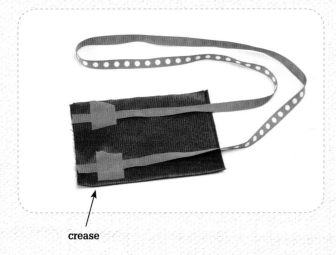

crease

2 Measure 1" (3cm) from the crease and tape one ribbon end. Measure 1" (3cm) from the right raw edge and tape on the other ribbon end. You may want to gather the excess ribbon and tape it in the center of the lining fabric to ensure it doesn't get caught in the stitching. Unfold.

3 Place the cover fabric on top of the lining with right sides together.

4 Serge along the top raw edge, ensuring the ribbon edges are caught in the stitching. Press the seam open.

5 Fold the pocket fabric in half with wrong sides together. Pin in place along the bottom of the cover fabric, at the opposite end of the ribbon.

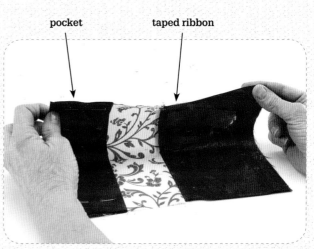

pocket   taped ribbon

6 Fold the cover and lining fabric lengthwise with right sides together. Be sure the pocket edges match and remain in place. Reposition the pins if necessary.

7 Fold in half again, this time crosswise. Pin in place. With raw edges to the left, serge along the bottom of all the layers.

8 Turn the lining to the outside. Ensure all seams are straight. Make sure the pocket is in place properly, not twisted. Pin in place. Serge through all the bottom layers.

9 Turn the purse right sides out and press the seams.

**Personalize
your purse**
Make your purse with
or without a pocket, and
use ribbon, cording or
even braiding for your
handle.

Remember to...
Clean your serger regularly. A
small cosmetic brush or even
a thin paintbrush works well to
remove bits of fluff.

Housewife Pillowcase

A few years ago, a friend from the UK sent me a housewife pillowcase. It was perfect to adapt to serger sewing. This type of pillowcase has a sewn flap on the open end. When a pillow is tucked into the case, this flap folds in to cover the pillow. No more unsightly pillow showing, and the flap stays tucked in.

Normally, a housewife pillowcase is made from one long length of fabric, but a colorful border is easy to add using three pieces of fabric. As fast as these stitch up, you can make several for your own bedroom and oodles more for gifts!

Materials

⁎ Case fabric: 20" × 42" (51cm × 107cm)

⁎ Border fabric*: 9" × 20" (23cm × 51cm)

⁎ Flap fabric: 18" × 20" (46cm × 51cm)

* Instead of having a border, you could make the pillowcase from one long 47" × 42" (119cm × 107cm) strip of fabric.

Serger settings

⁎ 3 or 4 thread overlock

⁎ **Stitch length:** 2 to 2.5mm

⁎ **Stitch width:** 5 to 6mm

⁎ **Cutting blade:** ON

⁎ **Differential feed:** Adjust as necessary

⁎ **Foot:** Standard serger foot

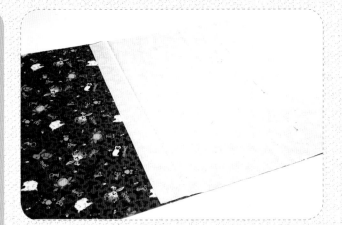

2 Place the 18" × 20" (46cm × 51cm) flap piece on the right side, with right sides together. Serge. Trim any excess threads. At this point, you will have one very long piece of fabric.

3 Serge both short ends to finish the edges.

4 Lay the fabric piece right side up, with the large flap to the right.

5 Fold the left side over, meeting the seams.

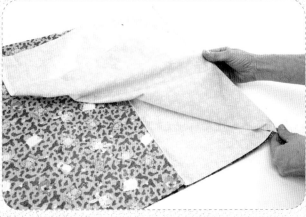

1 Place the 20" × 42" (51cm × 107cm) case piece face up. Place the 9" × 20" (23cm × 51cm) header piece on the left side, with right sides together. Serge. Trim any excess threads.

6 Fold the right side over. Pin in place.

7 Serge each side. Trim and secure any excess threads.

8 Turn the pillowcase right sides out and press. Place the pillow inside the case and tuck the flap over the top.

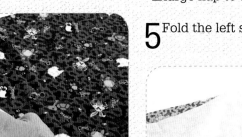

Stitch solution

Poor stitch formation may be caused by thread not seated correctly in the tension disks.

Nice save

Have a well-worn but loved vintage crocheted-edge pillowcase? Upcycle the crocheted section and make a new pillowcase.

Varying border lengths

Varying the border size is easy: Add inches (or centimeters) to the border piece, and deduct that amount from the case fabric. This is a great way to use up fabric scraps.

Coffee Cozy

Whether your drink of choice is latte or chai tea, your fingers will appreciate this stylish cozy. Add a small pocket for holding sugar and spare change, or a larger one for sticky notes and a pen for your next business meeting. The cozy's interlining keeps fingers from getting burned. A Velcro closure makes the cozy adjustable for various cup sizes. Use the pattern provided, or save the cardboard liner from your next to-go cup. For a wider pocket, adjust the size of the pocket piece. Use heat-resistant fabric or fleece as the interlining. Adjust the pattern width if necessary to fit your favorite cup.

Materials

* Cozy fabric: 7" × 14" (18cm × 36cm)
* Lining: 7" × 14" (18cm × 36cm)
* Heat-resistant interlining: 7" × 14" (18cm × 36cm)
* 4" (10cm) long piece of ⅝" to 1" (16mm to 25mm) wide Velcro (for closure)
* Cozy template (page 77)
* Optional: 5" × 6" (13cm × 15cm) pocket fabric
* Optional: Beads, piping, trims for embellishment

Serger settings

* 3 or 4 thread overlock
* **Stitch length:** 2.5 to 3mm
* **Stitch width:** 6mm
* **Cutting blade:** ON
* **Foot:** Standard serger foot (Optional: Multipurpose serger foot, beading foot)

1 Cut one each of the template out of the cozy fabric, lining and interlining.

2 If adding a pocket, fold the pocket piece in half right sides together. Serge the top and both sides. Turn right sides out and press.

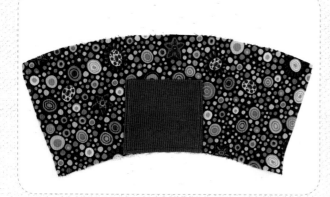

3 Place the pocket on the cozy fabric where desired, matching the bottom of the pocket and the bottom raw edge of cozy fabric. Head to your sewing machine and stitch the two side seams of the pocket in place—or, sew the pocket in place using the serger's cover stitch.

4 Place the cozy fabric and lining right sides together. Place the interlining on top of the fabric and lining. Pin in place.

5 Serge one short side and both long edges, leaving one short side open for turning. Use the wrapped corner method for less bulk (see page 42).

6 Turn right sides out and press. Fold the opening inward and press closed. Hand sew the opening or head to your sewing machine and top stitch very close to the edge.

7 Place the Velcro pieces (right side on one end, wrong side on the opposite end). Check to ensure they'll match when closed. Head to your sewing machine to stitch the Velcro in place.

Cozy template
Shown at 100%.

FOLD

(project shown completed by Megan McGuire)

Mix and match
Pull out your scrap fabrics to coordinate or
contrast your colors.

Girl's Ruffled Tank Top

Adding a ruffle to the bottom is a nice way to extend the life of a simple, outgrown T-shirt or tank top. Serge a cute, short ruffle to simply embellish the shirt, or add a longer ruffle and make a dress just perfect for your little princess. Materials for this project are sized for a 5-year-old, but you can easily adjust the width and length of the ruffle to fit any age or size. Simply measure the width of the bottom edge where you are attaching the ruffle, and cut a strip of fabric two and a half times this length.

Materials

* Tank top or T-shirt
* For ruffle on tank: one 4½" (11cm) wide piece, the width of the tank top
* For short ruffle on T-shirt: one 4½" (11cm) wide piece, width determined by width of shirt
* For longer ruffle on T-shirt: measure length desired and multiply by 2, plus add 2" (5cm) for seams
* To determine ruffle fabric width, measure the bottom of the T-shirt and multiply by 2.5

Serger settings

* 3 or 4 thread overlock
* **Stitch length:** 3 to 4mm
* **Stitch width:** 6mm
* **Cutting blade:** ON
* **Differential feed:** Adjust as necessary
* **Foot:** Standard serger foot

* 3 or 4 thread gathering
* **Stitch length:** 3 to 4mm
* **Stitch width:** 2.5 to 3mm
* **Cutting blade:** ON
* **Differential feed:** Adjust as necessary
* **Foot:** Gathering foot

1 Cut the hem from the shirt. Set the shirt aside.

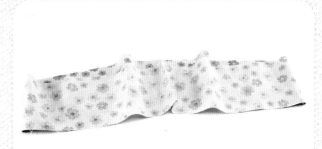

2 Set serger to overlock stitch. Fold the ruffle fabric crosswise, right sides together, and serge seam, forming a tube.

3 Turn right side out. Press the seam.

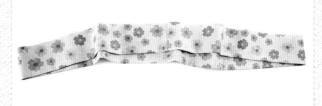

4 Fold in half lengthwise, wrong sides together. Press.

5 Set serger to gathering stitch. Serge the raw edges. The fabric will gather as you serge.

6 For additional fullness and fitting the ruffle to the bottom width of the shirt, locate the needle threads (see page 43) at the beginning or ending of the stitching. Pull the threads to fit. Adjust the gathers to distribute fullness.

Serger tip

Gathering is easy to do by using the flatlock stitch to sew over cord. Use the cording foot and set the machine for a 2- or 3-thread flatlock. Insert the cord into the guide of the cording foot, and flatlock over the cord. Pull on the cord to achieve the desired fullness.

7 Pin the gathered piece to the bottom edge of the shirt, right sides together. Remember to place the pins parallel to and away from the edge.

8 Set serger for construction stitch. Serge the ruffle to the shirt. Secure the ends and trim any excess thread.

Experiment with ruffle length
Ruffles can be just short enough to add a little hemline flair, or long enough to turn a shirt into a dress. Follow the same steps you did for the tank top, using the different measurements and settings for each on page 79.

Single-layer ruffle
Instead of folding the fabric lengthwise to make a double-layer ruffle, try gathering a single layer of fabric. Cut to the length needed, and hem the bottom using a rolled edge hem. Gather the top raw edge and stitch to the shirt.

Lunch Bag

Typically when we brown-bag it, we grab a small paper lunch bag. Be more eco-friendly and customize your lunch sack by making your own. Whether you make it from fabric or oilcloth, it will always be ready to use over and over. When it needs a quick cleanup, just toss it in the washer.

Materials

* Oilcloth/fabric: cut one 12" × 32" (30cm × 81cm), or if fabric is directional, cut two 12" × 16½" (30cm × 42cm)
* Lining: cut two 12" × 16" (30cm × 41cm)
* 7" (18cm) long piece of elastic cord
* Large button
* Optional: Velcro

Serger settings

* 3 or 4 thread overlock
* **Stitch length:** 2 to 2.5mm
* **Stitch width:** 6mm
* **Cutting blade:** ON
* **Differential feed:** Adjust as necessary to the oilcloth
* **Foot:** Standard serger foot

1 Fold the fabric in half, right sides together. Serge the sides. Secure and trim excess threads.

2 Place the lining pieces right sides together. Serge the sides. Secure and trim the excess threads. Set aside.

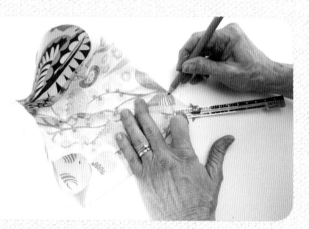

3 Fold one bottom corner of fabric at an angle, matching the side seam and bottom fold. Measure in 2" (5cm) and mark.

4 Serge the corner. Repeat for the remaining corner.

Serger tip

You could eliminate the lining and overcast the top edge using a decorative thread. When using decorative threads, there can be a tendency for stitches to pile up under the presser foot. To prevent this, clear the stitch fingers before serging.

5 Turn the fabric piece right side out. Lightly press the seams. Tape elastic cord in the middle of the top raw edge.

6 Slide the lining piece over the fabric piece, right sides together. Match the side seams and top raw edges. Pin in place.

7 Serge the top edge. Secure and trip the excess threads.

8 Pull the lining out into one long piece. Serge the bottom. Stitch each corner following the instructions in steps 3 and 4.

9 Slide the lining into the fabric. Mark the spot for the button and sew it on.

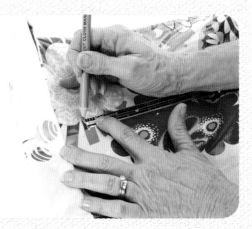

For a fold-over top
If you would rather close the top edge by folding it over several times, use Velcro for the closure. Fold the serged top edge down several times. Mark the placement for the Velcro strips. Head to your sewing machine and sew the Velcro in place.

Make serger buttons
Make serger buttons quickly and easily to decorate your lunch bag. Draw triangles on two 3" × 7" (8cm × 18cm) pieces of fabric. Place wrong sides together and serge the two long ends. Apply sealant, let dry, and clip any excess threads. Apply fabric glue to one side of the triangle. Starting at the edge opposite the point, roll each triangle into a tube, then glue the point in place. The button size will vary depending on the width you cut the fabric. Try various widths.

Punch of color

A simple black and white bag punctuated with a bright button sets an elegant yet fun tone.

Smaller bags

Make a sandwich bag to match your lunch sack. Cut one piece of fabric 7" × 14" (18cm × 36cm) and two pieces of lightweight vinyl 7" × 7½" (18cm × 19cm). Follow the directions for the lunch bag to stitch, and add Velcro to close. Now you're ready to put your sandwich inside and go! Adjust the material sizes to make a smaller snack sack.

Get a handle on it

Use your sewing machine to add a handle, with a matching strip for a Velcro closure. Stitch the handle and strip before assembling.

Handle detail

Topstitch the handles. Add double rows of stitching for durability.

85

Piped Pillow

Don't just make a plain pillow when you can easily embellish the front with piping. Use pieces of contrasting fabric for a fun and scrappy pillow. Use your piping foot for this fast project (finished size: about 12" × 16" [30cm × 41cm]). Instead of creating your own piping with the serger, you can head to the sewing machine to make your piping. Then use your serger to insert the piping between the fabric. Commercially covered piping can also be used.

(project shown completed by Megan McGuire)

Materials

* Pillow front fabric: two 4½" × 18" (12cm × 46cm), one 7" × 18" (18cm × 46cm)
* Pillow back fabric: 13" × 18" (33cm × 46cm)
* Bias strips*: two 22" (56cm) in length, with width equal to the circumference of cording plus 1½" (4cm)
* Cording: 3.2mm, 66" (168cm) long
* Filling

* To make your own bias strips, cut them on the bias of the fabric. The width will be the circumference of the cord, plus 1½" (4cm) for seam allowance.

Serger settings

* 3 or 4 thread overlock
* **Stitch length:** 2.5mm
* **Stitch width:** 6mm
* **Cutting blade:** ON
* **Differential feed:** Adjust as necessary
* **Foot:** Piping foot
  (Optional: Multipurpose foot)

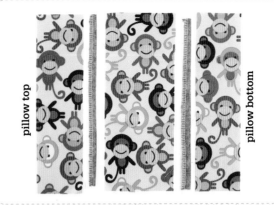

pillow top

pillow bottom

3 Each piping strip will be placed between two fabric pieces to create the front of the pillow.

4 Place a small section of the pillow front fabric right side up under the piping strip. Serge. Remove from the machine.

5 Place the second section of the pillow front fabric (the largest piece) facedown on top of the completed first section. Insert both layers under the serger foot so the piping lies in the groove. Serge. Trim the excess cords. Repeat for the last section. Press the seams.

6 Pin the finished front piece to the back piece, right sides together, raw edges even. Serge, leaving a 5" (13cm) opening. Turn right side out and lightly press the seams. Stuff with filling. Hand stitch the opening closed.

1 Lower the needles, raise the presser foot, and insert the cording into the tape guide and under the left side of the foot. Lower the presser foot and take a few stitches to secure the cording.

2 Raise the foot and wrap the bias strip around the cording. Be sure the cord is under the groove of the foot. Serge. Repeat for the other bias strips.

Remember to...
Ensure that construction seams will hide the stitches made when creating the covered piping. Use the right needle when making piping; use the left when inserting the piping.

Make a zippered pillow cover

Like to change out your pillow colors throughout the year? Quickly make a pillow cover with an exposed zipper. Place your pillow inside for a quick change of colors and designs. Measure your pillow and add 2" (5cm) to each seam. Select a zipper that is at least 4" (10cm) longer than your pillow. Follow the instructions on page 93 to quickly add a zipper with your serger.

For mini-piping

Create a small mini-piping to use as an accent on garments. Set the serger for 2- or 3-thread overlock with the right needle. Cut bias strips and fold the strips in half with a small cord inside the fold (or try perle cotton or Pearl crown rayon). Serge over the fold.

Pillowcase piping

Now that you know how to make piping, try using it to embellish the housewife pillowcase (see page 72). Add it to your border before sewing to the case fabric.

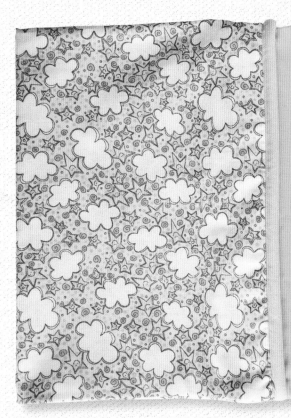

Travel Neck Pillow

Whether traveling by car or plane, don't arrive with a sore, stiff neck. Use your serger to make a personal neck pillow. It's so comfortable, you will have to make one for everyone in your family! The serger is great for gentle curves, but take it slow. This template makes a medium-size pillow. For larger or smaller neck sizes, adjust the size of the circle accordingly.

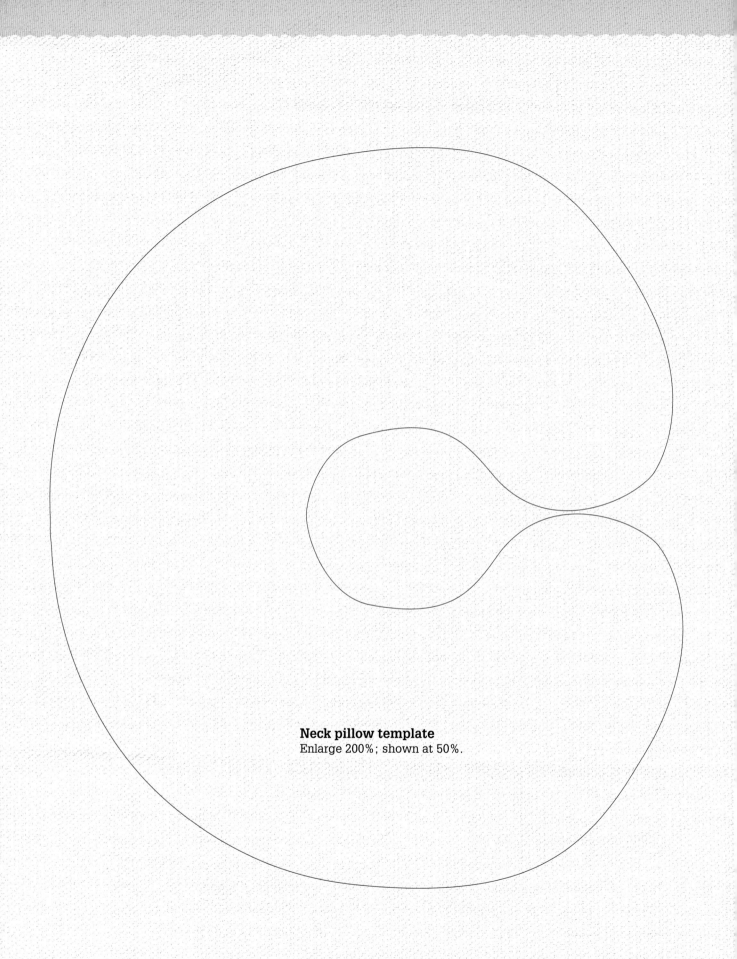

Neck pillow template
Enlarge 200%; shown at 50%.

Materials

* Pillow fabric: two 15" × 16" (38cm × 41cm)
* Filling
* Pillow template (page 90)

Serger settings

* 3 or 4 thread overlock
* **Stitch length:** 2.5mm
* **Stitch width:** 6mm
* **Cutting blade:** ON
* **Differential feed:** Adjust as necessary
* **Foot:** Standard serger foot

Serger tip

If the serger seams are visible on the right side, the needle tension(s) may be too loose. Check to make sure the threads are seated in the tension disks properly, and increase the tension(s) if necessary.

1 Cut the fabric (two pieces, front and back) according to the pillow template.

2 Place the fabric pieces right sides together. Serge, going slowly around the curves. Leave a 5" (13cm) opening. Angle off, leaving at least a 6" (15cm) tail.

3 Turn right side out and lightly press the seams.

4 Stuff with filler. Don't overstuff or the pillow will be too firm.

5 Fold over the edges of the opening and pin in place. Hand sew opening closed.

Cosmetics Bag

It's hard to believe the history of cosmetics spans around six thousand years of our history. For centuries, women have been making small bags to carry those special items. After creating one or two from this particular design, you'll be able to custom-make any size that fits your needs. Use contrasting fabric or place your zipper diagonally for a unique effect.

Materials

* Fabric: 8½" × 14" (22cm × 36cm)
* 12" (30cm) nylon zipper (NOT metal)
* Ribbon: 4" (10cm) long, ⅛" to ¼" (3mm to 6mm) wide
* Marking pencil

Serger settings

* 3 or 4 thread overlock
* **Stitch length:** 2.5 to 3mm
* **Stitch width:** 5 to 7mm
* **Cutting blade:** ON
* **Foot:** Cording foot
  (Optional: Standard serger foot, multipurpose foot)

Zipper tips

✂ The teeth of the zipper fit into the groove on the bottom of the cording foot, giving a very nice, straight seam. A standard serger foot can be used, sewing slowing to keep zipper teeth parallel from edge of fabric.

✂ Line the zipper edge with the cutting guide, but do not cut into the zipper and most of the zipper shows. If you would rather see less of the zipper tape, place so the cutting guide cuts about ⅛" (3mm) of the zipper tape.

✂ When serging the side seams, be sure to open zipper. Don't accidentally cut off the zipper pull! Learn from my experience.

1 Open the zipper, and with right sides together, center it along one shorter edge of the fabric. The zipper should extend beyond each side about 2" (5cm).

2 Place the zipper under the cording foot, lining up the teeth of the zipper in the groove of the cording foot. Serge. Trim the excess fabric.

3 Close the zipper and make placement marks on the zipper to indicate the fabric edge.

4 Open the zipper. On the opposite side of the fabric, with right sides of the zipper together, align the placement marks. Serge the zipper to the fabric.

5 Close the zipper. Fold the fabric, right sides together, with the zipper about 1" to 1½" (3cm to 4cm) below the top fold. This places the zipper not at the top of the bag, but just a little below. Pin in place.

6 With right sides together, serge along the edge where the bottom of the zipper is located. Stitch slowly over the zipper teeth, cutting off the excess zipper. Secure and trim any excess threads.

7 Open the zipper about 3" (8cm) and serge along the opposite side of the bag. Secure and trim the excess threads.

8 Turn the bag right side out through the zipper opening. Tie a small ribbon or add a charm to the zipper pull and it's ready to use.

Make a tassel
Make a tassel using the serger's chainstitch or rolled hem stitch. Serge about 8 to 10 yards (7.3 to 9.1 meters) of thread chain to make "yarn." Wrap the thread around a 3" (8cm) width of cardboard. Place seam sealant along one edge. Let dry.

Using the beginning and end of the thread chain, tie loops around the opposite edge. Slide off the cardboard. Cut the end with the seam sealant. Wrap the tied end with more thread tail and tie off.

Add piping
Insert a separate serged or commercial piping between the fabric and the zipper tape for a unique finish.

Beautiful bag lady
Make your bag from 100-percent cotton, or try quilted fabric or upholstery fabric for a sturdier bag. Dress up your zipper pulls with ribbons, tassels and playful charms.

(quilted bags shown below completed by Megan McGuire)

Three-Ring Pencil Pouch

Serge a one-of-a-kind pencil carrier to keep all your writing implements handy yet conveniently tucked away in a three-ring binder. Choose your fabric and zipper color to spice up an ordinary-looking binder. Use grommets for a nice, durable touch, or head to your sewing machine and make eyelets. Instead of constructing your pouch from fabric only, add some vinyl to the front.

Materials

* Fabric: two 11" × 15" (28cm × 38cm)
* Medium-weight fusible stabilizer: 11" × 15" (28cm × 38cm)
* Polyester zipper: 18" to 22" (46cm to 56cm) long
* Grommets: three ⅜" (10mm) in diameter
* Marking pencil
* Optional: 4 yards (4m) binding, eyelets

Serger settings

* **3 or 4 thread narrow overlock**
* **Stitch length:** 2mm
* **Stitch width:** 5 to 7mm
* **Cutting blade:** ON
* **Differential feed:** Adjust as necessary
* **Foot:** Cording foot (Optional: Standard serger foot, multipurpose foot)

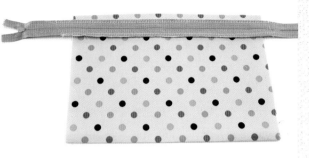

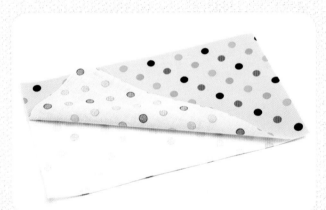

1 Fuse stabilizer to the wrong side of one 11" × 15" (28cm × 38cm) piece. Place the second fabric on top, with wrong sides together.

2 Insert the zipper following the instructions for cosmetics bag (see pages 93–94).

3 With right sides together, fold the zipper down ¾" to 1" (19mm to 25mm) from the top.

4 Serge the two side seams and turn the pouch right sides out.

5 Lay the pencil pouch to the right of the rings on a three-ring notebook and mark accordingly for the grommets (or eyelets). Add grommets according to the manufacturer's instructions, or head to your sewing machine to add eyelets.

Grommets

Grommets are durable and easy to add to any sewing project. They are available in sizes ranging from 3/16" to 1½" (5mm to 4cm), in brass or stainless steel finishes. A grommet kit includes all the necessary tools to install.

Prevent wavy seams

Stabilize seams on stretchy fabrics to prevent "waves." Serge over water-soluble stabilizer placed over the seam line, or stitch through lightweight paper and rip from the seam when finished.

Couched Necklace

There's no need to head to the jewelry store when you can make a versatile necklace yourself at home. Couch over cord to make a quick, simple and personalized necklace. Select some decorative beads or a pendant to slide on. Switch out the beads or pendant on occasion for any look that you need.

Materials

* Cord: 3.2mm, 30" (76cm) long (NOTE: I have used satin rat tail)
* Beads large enough to slide over the knotted end
* Decorative thread

Serger settings

* **2 or 3 thread overlock**
* **Stitch length:** 1.5 to 2mm
* **Stitch width:** N/A when using cording or multipurpose foot
* **Cutting blade:** OFF
* **Differential feed:** Adjust as necessary
* **Foot:** Cording foot
  (Optional: Multipurpose foot)

1 Thread the serger with decorative thread in the upper looper.

2 Place the cord under the groove of the foot so that the needle is to the left of the cord. Pull the cord behind the presser foot at least 1" (3cm).

4 Tie a knot in one end of the cord. Tie a looped end on the opposite end of the cord. A small dab of glue can help secure tied ends. (If you are a great jewelry crafter, you will find numerous other ways to secure the ends.)

3 Serge over the cord, holding the thread tails behind the foot (don't pull). Stop and adjust the stitch length so the cord is completely enclosed.

5 Slide a pendant or beads on and off as desired.

Cording tips

✂ If using cording smaller than 3.2mm, pull the serger's rolled hem lever toward you (if available on your machine).

✂ Use the right needle for smaller cord, and the left needle for larger cording.

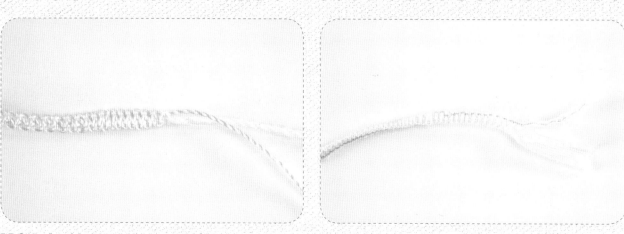

Make a braid

Use your 3- or 4-thread overlock stitch and a strip of tricot to quickly make a braid. Cut the tricot to about ¾" (19mm) wide. Adjust the stitch width to encase the tricot while stitching. Use the finished braid as an embellishment, such as adding to a sleeve edge.

Try it

Try using satin rat-tail cording for a glamorous base under serger stitches. The cord acts like a stabilizer to keep the looper threads from unraveling.

Add beads

Try stringing beads onto your necklace instead of a pendant.

Ruffled Waist Apron

Grandma's apron was used for so many things—wiping her hands, drying tears, and pulling hot pans from the oven. The pockets were handy as she went through the house picking up items here and there, or for holding her handkerchief. Make an apron of your own with a gather at the bottom, and use your serger to quickly fashion the waistband ties.

(project shown completed by Megan McGuire)

Materials

* Apron body fabric: 18" × 21" (46cm × 53cm)
* Waistband fabric: 3" × 21" (8cm × 53cm)
* Apron ties: two 3" × 36" long (8cm × 91cm)
* Ruffle fabric: 6" × 32" (15cm × 81cm); if using lace, 3" × 32" (8cm × 81cm)

Serger settings

(for gathering)

* 3 or 4 thread gathering
* **Stitch length:** 3 to 4mm
* **Stitch width:** 6 to 9mm
* **Cutting blade:** ON
* **Differential feed:** Adjust as necessary
* **Foot:** Standard serger foot (Optional: gathering foot)

(for rolled edge hem)

* 2 or 3 thread rolled edge
* **Stitch length:** 1mm
* **Stitch width:** 5 to 6mm
* **Cutting blade:** ON
* **Differential feed:** Adjust as necessary
* **Foot:** Standard serger foot

(for narrow overlock stitch)

* 3 or 4 thread narrow overlock
* **Stitch length:** 2.5mm
* **Stitch width:** 5 to 6mm
* **Cutting blade:** ON
* **Differential feed:** Adjust as necessary
* **Foot:** Standard serger foot

1 Set serger to rolled hem stitch. Serge a rolled hem along one long edge of the ruffle strip.

2 Set serger to gathering stitch. Serge the top edge of the ruffle. Find the needle threads (see page 43), and pull gathers to fit the bottom width of the apron body.

3 Set serger to narrow overlock stitch. Pin the gathered strip to the bottom of the apron body. Serge.

Another option

Eliminate the rolled edge hem. Instead of using a single layer of fabric for the ruffle, double the width of the ruffle when cutting. Fold in half lengthwise, with wrong sides together. Gather and attach following the instructions on page 79.

5 Make each apron tie following the instructions for making a tube (see page 50).

6 Place one apron tie on the inside of the waistband, matching raw edges. Pin to secure. Repeat with the second tie for the other side.

7 Serge from the top of the waistband to the bottom of the ruffle. Secure and cut off the excess threads.

4 Fold the waistband fabric in half lengthwise, with wrong sides together. Pin to the top of the apron body. Serge. Trim the excess threads.

Serger tip

If your machine has differential feed, practice gathering by setting the differential feed to 1.0 or 2.0.

103

E-Reader Cover

No E-reader is complete without protection. Instead of buying a standard cover, make one to fit your personality. Tuck notes and pencils into the pocket and have everything ready to grab and go.

Materials

* Fabric: two 7" × 9¼" (18cm × 23cm)
* Lining: two 7" × 9¼" (18cm × 23cm)
* Fleece lining: two 7" × 9¼" (18cm × 23cm)
* Pocket: 7" × 10" (18cm × 25cm)
* Flap: 3¾" × 6" (9cm × 15cm)
* 2" (5cm) long piece of Velcro

Serger settings

* 3 or 4 thread overlock
* Stitch length: 2.5mm
* Stitch width: 6mm
* Cutting blade: ON
* Differential feed: Adjust as necessary
* Foot: Standard serger foot

5 Serge the layers on the sides and bottom. Turn right sides out, and lightly press the seams.

6 Pin the flap to the top back of the fabric layers, matching raw edges (on the side opposite the pocket).

1 Fold the flap in half, right sides together. Serge each side. Trim excess threads. Turn to the right side and press, then set aside.

2 Place the lining pieces right sides together. Serge each long side, then set aside.

3 Fold the pocket in half lengthwise, wrong sides together. Press lightly.

7 Slide the lining over the layers, wrong sides out and matching the side seams and the top raw edge. Pin in place.

8 Serge the lining to the layers at the top raw edge.

9 Slide the lining off the layers and lay the cover straight.

4 Layer the pieces in this order: fleece, fabric right side up, pocket, fabric right side down, fleece.

10 Serge the lining bottom.

11 Slide the lining inside the cover.

12 Slide your Kindle, Nook or other E-reader inside and determine how snug you want it to close. Mark the placement for Velcro on the main body and flap.

13 Head to your sewing machine and stitch the Velcro in place. Hand sew a button, flower or even a yo-yo to hide any stitches.

Dress it up
Embellish the E-reader cover with embroidery, appliqué, beads or buttons.

Fold-Up Tote

Reusable totes have been around for several years as an easy way to go green. Quickly make one or more and personalize it to make it fit your style. Add a pocket and fold up the bag to tuck into your purse. Make several bags and place gifts inside—giving your family two gifts in one! Try using oilcloth, or add a lining.

Materials

* Tote body: 18" × 40" (46cm × 102cm); if print is directional, two 18" × 20" (46cm × 51cm)
* Handles: two 5½" × 18" (14cm × 46cm)
* Marking pencil
* Optional: 8½" × 11" (22cm × 28cm) tote pocket

Serger settings

* 3 or 4 thread overlock
* **Stitch length:** 2 to 2.5mm
* **Stitch width:** 5 to 6mm
* **Cutting blade:** ON
* **Differential feed:** Adjust as necessary
* **Foot:** Standard serger foot

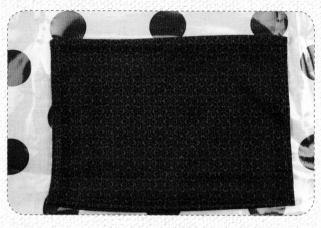

2 Fold the tote piece in half lengthwise. Lightly press the fold. Unfold. Measure 2" (5cm) up from the fold and mark. Place the bottom of the pocket along the mark, and in the center of the fabric. Topstitch in place using your sewing machine or the serger's cover stitch.

3 Fold the fabric right sides together. Serge both side edges.

1 Fold the pocket right sides together. Serge around each side. Secure and trim away the excess threads. Turn right sides out and press. Fold the opening under ¼" (6mm) and press.

4 Fold each bottom corner diagonally, having bottom and side seams meet. Measure 2" (5cm) from the tip and mark. Serge. Repeat for the other side.

5 For each handle, place right sides together lengthwise and sew as for a tube (see page 50). Lightly press.

6 Place one handle 3½" (9cm) from the side edge. Pin in place. Repeat for other handle. Serge the top of the bag, catching the handles in the stitching.

(see page 50)

For extra-durable handles

If you want additional durability for the handles, head to your sewing machine and topstitch the top edge after serging.

Serger tip

Use the cover stitch for topstitching. If the looper threads are to be visible, place the outside of the project next to the feed dogs, facedown. If the needle threads are to be visible, place the outside of the project face up.

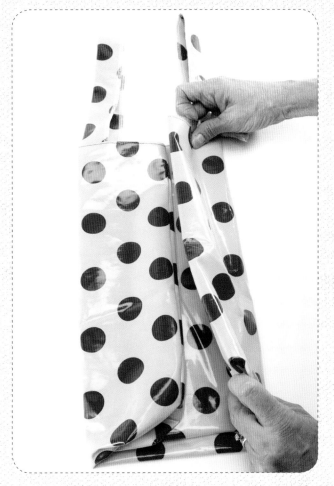

Fold and stow

When you're ready to put the bag away, bring the left and right sides to the center. Flip it over, fold the tote down, and tuck into the pocket. Toss in your purse for your next shopping trip!

Fabric options
You could choose a variety of batiks for a scrappy look, or try denim for a heavier tote.

Two totes in one
Add a lining to make a reversible tote.

Flat Iron Travel Case

Flat irons have been around since the early 1900s, and although they have substantially improved since then, the same dilemma remains: How do you pack a hot iron? This travel case utilizes heat-resistant fabric to end that "waiting to cool" time before you pack. Even if not traveling, having a heat-resistant case is handy for quickly tucking that hot iron away from small children in the house.

Materials

✳ Main fabric: one 6" × 22" (15cm × 56cm), one 6" × 16⅝" (15cm × 42cm), one 6" × 12¾" (15cm × 32cm)

✳ Silver heat-resistant fabric: one 6" × 22" (15cm × 56cm), one 6" × 16⅝" (15cm × 42cm)

✳ Ribbon: two 12" (30cm) pieces

✳ Optional: Binding

Serger settings

✳ 3 or 4 thread overlock

✳ **Stitch length:** 2.5 to 3mm

✳ **Stitch width:** 6 to 7mm

✳ **Cutting blade:** ON

✳ **Differential feed:** 1.5 to 2mm, adjust as necessary

✳ **Foot:** Standard serger foot

2 Place the 6" × 16⅝" (15cm × 42cm) fabric piece and 6" × 16⅝" (15cm × 42cm) heat-resistant fabric right sides together. Serge along one short end. Trim the excess threads. Turn right sides out and press the seam. Fold on the seam line.

3 Place the layers from step 1 fabric side up. Place the layer from step 3 fabric side down to the layers, with the silver side facing up and matching raw edges.

1 Layer the 6" × 22" (15cm × 56cm) main fabric right side up over the 6" × 22" (15cm × 56cm) heat-resistant fabric silver-side down. Place ribbon in the center of each end and tape in place. Set aside.

4 Fold the 6" × 12¾" (15cm × 32cm) fabric piece in half, wrong sides together. Lightly press. Place at the opposite end of the layers, matching raw edges and having the fold toward the inside. Round off the two corners at the raw edge.

Tips

✂ Heat-resistant fabric is available in silver and tan, or with a quilted embossed design.

✂ Instead of ribbons, add a buttonhole and button or Velcro for closing.

5 Serge all the way around. Secure and trim any excess threads.

6 Turn right sides out.

7 Fold the flap down and tie closed.

Make a cord bag

Worried about packing the electric cord directly next to the hot iron? Make a quick case for the cord. Cut a 4" × 10" (10cm × 25cm) piece of heat-resistant fabric. Serge one short end. Cut the excess thread tails. Fold in half lengthwise, with the silver inside. Serge the side and the bottom. Turn right side out.

Thread Catcher Mat

Fabric strips left after a serger cut quickly pile up. Serge your own thread catcher mat, for placing under your serger and keeping them from becoming a mess. Add some pockets and a detachable pin cushion for storing your notions. Most quilted fabrics have contrasting designs on each side that follow the same color scheme. Here, one pattern appears under the serger, and the contrasting pattern forms the drop with the serger pocket. Have loads of contrasting fabric and quilt batting? Quilt your own fabric and then start serging!

Materials

* Quilted fabric: about ½ yard (.5m), or 18" × 42" (46cm × 107cm) (entire piece will be used)
* Matching or contrasting fabric: 22½" × 11½" (57cm × 29cm), for pocket
* Heavyweight interfacing: 11" × 11" (28cm × 28cm)
* Optional: 7" × 7" (18cm × 18cm) clear vinyl, for smaller pocket and scissor pocket
* Optional: Two 6" × 6" (15cm × 15cm) fabric squares, stuffing and Velcro for pin cushion

Serger settings

* 3 or 4 thread overlock
* **Stitch length:** 2.5 to 3mm
* **Stitch width:** 5 to 7mm
* **Cutting blade:** ON
* **Differential feed:** Adjust as necessary
* **Foot:** Standard serger foot

1 Place your quilted fabric lengthwise.

2 Serge the top and bottom edges of the quilted fabric (the two short ends).

3 Most quilted fabrics have a different matching design on each side. Choose which pattern you wish to have facing up and showing while under the serger. Fold one-third of the quilted fabric down (the side facing up as you fold is the pattern you chose to be under the serger). Pin in place.

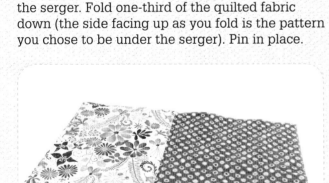

4 Serge both longer side edges, catching the top folded piece. Your piece will now have an approximate 12" (30cm) drop, and the fabric under the serger is a double layer.

5 Prepare the thread catcher pocket. Fold the pocket fabric in half lengthwise, right sides together. Serge each side seam. Turn right sides out and press. Slide the interfacing into the bottom edge of the pocket.

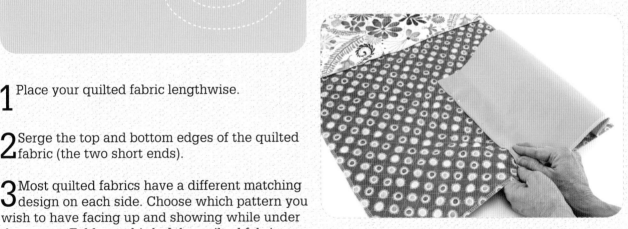

6 Measure 2" (5cm) from the right side of the quilted fabric. Pin one side of the pocket in place, with the folded edge toward the top. Measure 10" (25cm) from the opposite fabric edge and pin the other side of the pocket in place. There should be a nice bulge to hold your scraps.

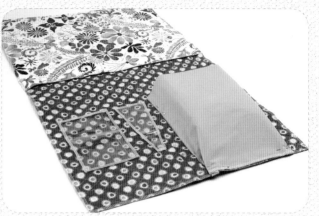

7 Keeping each pocket side edge straight, fold the bottom of the pocket up about 1" (3cm). You will need to make a fold in the pocket to maintain the bulge. Pin in place.

8 Head to your sewing machine and stitch the bottom and sides of the pocket in place, or use the serger's cover stitch.

9 To make the rectangular vinyl pocket, cut the vinyl into a 3" × 6" (8cm × 15cm) rectangle. Serge along all four edges. Determine the placement on the thread catcher and sew in place using your sewing machine (or use the serger's cover stitch). (See the sidebar on page 121.)

10 Cut a vinyl piece in a "V" shape to fit small scissors. Serge along all its edges. Determine the placement and pin in place. Sew the two long "V" edges in place with your sewing machine, or use the serger's cover stitch.

All finished! Place under your serger, add your tools and scissors, and you are ready to catch all those scraps and keep your tools at hand. Remember the double layer of quilted fabric under your serger? The right side is a handy place to tuck small tools into.

Optional pin cushion
Sew Velcro to the right side of one of the 6" (15cm) squares, centering it. Place the two squares right sides together and serge three sides. Stuff and hand sew the remaining side closed. Sew the opposite Velcro piece to the back of the thread catcher, near the top on the right side.

Making your own quilted fabric

Quilted fabric can be purchased commercially or custom made. Choose a low-loft batting for the thread catcher when making your own quilted fabric.

Candleholder Centerpiece

Add style and fun to your next outdoor meal! Make these colorful candle surrounds in several sizes to help set a festive table. For safety, the candles placed inside should be within glass containers or votives and positioned a safe distance from the candleholder's fabric sides, or try using flameless candles. No matter the candle size, your table will certainly glow.

(project shown completed by Megan McGuire)

Materials

* Fabric: eight 6" × 6" (15cm × 15cm) pieces
* Stabilizer: four 6" × 6" (15cm × 15cm) pieces
* Glue stick

Serger settings

* 2 or 3 thread rolled hem, or 3 or 4 thread narrow overlock
* **Stitch length:** 1 to 2mm
* **Stitch width:** 5 to 6mm
* **Cutting blade:** ON
* **Differential feed:** Adjust as necessary
* **Foot:** Standard serger foot

1 Place one fabric piece wrong side up. Glue on the stabilizer. Place another fabric piece right side up, gluing in place. Repeat for the remaining pieces.

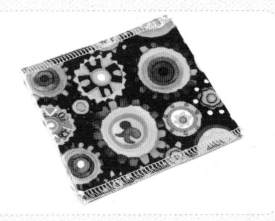

2 Serge the top and bottom of each fabric square using the rolled edge stitch or a narrow 3- or 4-thread overlock stitch. Cut the thread tails.

Serger tip

Place a shim or thick cardboard behind the presser foot when starting to sew very thick fabrics or stabilizer. This prevents thread buildup when beginning to serge. A shim also works well when serging over thick intersected seams.

Make a photo cube

Cut the same pieces of fabric and stabilizer as for the candleholder, plus four pieces of clear vinyl. Follow the candleholder instructions, but layer and serge only the top edge of each section. Now, place a piece of vinyl on top of each fabric section and serge the bottom edge (see the sidebar on page 121). Repeat for all sections. Then serge the sections together in the same way as for the candleholder. Slide in your photos and enjoy!

3 Place two squares together and serge the raw edge. Repeat with the remaining sides to form a cube. Secure the stitches and trim the excess thread. Place a glass-contained or flameless candle in the center. If you need to keep the bugs away, use a Citronella candle.

Gift or Luggage Tag

Give your gifts an extra-special touch! Write the recipient's name on tagboard and slide it under the vinyl. They can slide out the gift card and slip in a card with their name and contact information—turning their gift into a luggage tag. Now they have a unique tag on their luggage to distinguish it from hundreds of others.

Materials

* Fabric: 4" × 10" (10cm × 25cm)
* Lightweight stabilizer: 4" × 5" (10cm × 13cm)
* Clear vinyl front: 4" × 4" (10cm × 10cm)
* Ribbon: 14" (36cm) length
* Binding: two 1½" × 6" (4cm × 15cm) pieces
* Grommet or buttonhole
* Glue stick
* Marking pencil

Serger settings

* 3 or 4 thread narrow overlock
* **Stitch length:** 2.5mm
* **Stitch width:** 6mm
* **Cutting blade:** ON
* **Foot:** Standard serger foot

2 Place the side of the vinyl piece in between the binding folds, and glue it down. You can also topstitch with the sewing machine if you wish.

3 Place stabilizer down. Lay one half of the fabric right side up on top of the stabilizer. Place the vinyl on next, with the bound edge toward the fold and matching all raw edges. Fold the other half of the fabric on top, right side down.

4 Serge the two side edges. Trim the excess threads.

5 Turn right sides out and lightly press (not too hot, or you will damage the vinyl).

1 Press one of the binding pieces ¼" (6mm) in on each long side, wrong sides together. Fold in half lengthwise and press.

Working with vinyl

Vinyl is a slippery fabric and needs to be guided carefully through the serger. Gently pull behind the presser foot. Depending on your project, stabilizer can be placed between the vinyl and the presser foot to move it smoothly under the serger.

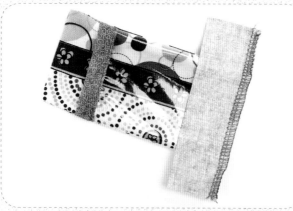

6 Place the right side of the binding to the right side of the tag, left edge. Serge the raw edge.

9 Measure to the middle of the top for the grommet, and mark.

10 Add the grommet according to the manufacturer's instructions (or add a buttonhole).

11 Tie the ribbon ends together.

12 Slide through the grommet.

7 Fold the binding to the back side. Fold up each serged bottom edge. Glue in place. Fold each end over. Glue in place to hold.

8 Fold the top down and fold down again to cover the raw edge. Hand sew in place.

Tissue Box Cover

I try to buy facial tissue boxes to match the room's color scheme. Not always easy. Now I quickly create the colors I need, even changing covers with the seasons. After doing several, I remembered seeing the small travel ones in my mother's craft magazines from thirty or forty years ago. Of course, those were sewn with a sewing machine. Now it's time to let your serger take center stage!

Materials

* Fabric: two 13" × 17" (33cm × 43cm) pieces

Serger settings

* 3 or 4 thread overlock
* **Stitch length:** 2 to 2.5mm
* **Stitch width:** 5 to 6mm
* **Cutting blade:** ON
* **Differential feed:** 1.5; adjust as necessary
* **Foot:** Standard serger foot

Serger tip

Keep an eye on your thread while serging. If you see a thread cone beginning to run low, stop and tie on thread from a new cone. Remember, the tied ends will go through the upper and lower looper easily. Never tie on the needle threads.

1 Place the two fabric pieces wrong sides together. Serge along the two short ends.

2 Find the middle by folding in half the matching serged ends. Mark the center. Fold over each serged end ¾" (19mm) and press. Bring each end to the center with serged ends up. Pin in place.

3 Serge the two shorter ends.

4 Turn the cover right side out and insert a tissue box.

Play with the fabric
The tissue holder uses little fabric and serves quickly, so time to practice serger techniques. Before serging the holder, play around with the fabric. Cut it into several pieces and add piping (page 87); jazz up with pintucks (page 18). If you are a quilter, create a patchwork fabric.

Tissues to go
Make a travel tissue holder to toss in your tote. Cut two fabric pieces 7½" × 5¼" (19cm × 13cm), and follow the same instructions as for the regular-size tissue cover. For larger travel tissue packs, cut two 6½" × 9" (17cm × 23cm) pieces instead.

Pajama Bottoms

Combine the various serger techniques you've learned with a commercial pattern. Some commercial patterns are perfect for sergers, when we think about methods used by the garment industry. The pieces are kept as flat as possible, for as long as possible. Remember, always think "serger sewing."

Materials

* Commercial pajama bottom pattern with elastic waistband*

* Fabric: Yardage according to your pattern

* Elastic: 1" (3cm) wide, length equal to your waist measurement plus 1" (3cm)

* Marking pencil

* Check your pattern to determine how the waistband is constructed. If the pattern has the waistband built into the front and back pieces (and not a separate piece), fold this section down when cutting. The instructions will explain how to stitch a separate waistband for ease in construction.

Serger settings

* 3 or 4 thread overlock
* **Stitch length:** 2.5mm
* **Stitch width:** 6mm
* **Cutting blade:** ON
* **Foot:** Standard serger foot

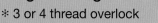

1 Cut and mark the fabric according to your pattern instructions. To reduce confusion during construction, now is the time to mark each piece as "front" and "back." Also remember to check the waistband. If it's built into the front and back pieces, fold this section down while cutting.

2 Serge the back side seam to the front side seam.

3 Repeat for the other side.

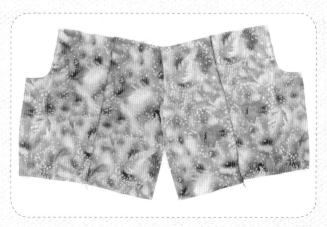

4 Match and serge the two front seams at the center crotch only. At this point, the pieces could be laid out flat and from left to right—back piece, front piece, front piece, and back piece.

5 Place with the crotch areas facing out. Measure and mark the hemline. If there is more than 1" (3cm) beyond the hemline, cut off the excess. Serge along the bottom of each leg section with the overlock stitch or a rolled edge hem.

Instead of cutting a waistband…

Try creating a folded casing by following these steps:

1. Fold the fabric at the waistband line, right sides together.
2. Fold the raw edge up, in half, with wrong sides together, folding away from you.
3. Serge along the fold, catching both the fold and the raw edge in the stitches. Serge and trim the excess threads.

6 If your pattern didn't have a separate waistband piece, cut one at this point. Measure the width of the waistline along the raw edges. Cut a strip this measurement and 3" (8cm) tall. Fold the waistband in half lengthwise, with wrong sides together. Press.

7 Place the right side of the waistband with the right side of the pants. Pin in place, then serge. Press the seams.

10 Fold the pants so that the center crotch seam matches in front and back. Match the bottom of each leg. Pin in place. Pin along each leg to secure in place. At this point, it begins to look like a pair of pants.

11 Begin at the bottom of one pant leg and serge up to and over the crotch seam, and down the other pant leg. Secure and trim the excess threads.

12 Turn the pants right sides out and press the seams.

8 Insert your elastic into the casing with a bodkin or safety pin. The elastic will extend at least ¼" (6mm) past each edge. Pin to secure.

9 With right sides together, match the back crotch area. Serge. Trim the excess threads.

Serger tip

When serging any curves, such as the crotch area, go very slowly around the curve. Also ensure that the serger cuts excess fabric throughout the seam to avoid skipped stitching. When serging the sharpest corner of the crotch area, it may help to periodically stop, raise the presser foot, adjust the fabric, lower the presser foot, and continue serging.

Quilted Tablerunner

Use your serger to piece and quilt at the same time. Begin with the center blocks and work your way outward until you reach the finished size. A serger makes quick work of a tablerunner, wall hanging, lap quilt, or even a larger bed-size quilt. Through the layering of fabrics and batting, you are sewing and quilting your work together all in one step. All that remains is to add the binding!

(project shown completed by Megan McGuire)

130

Materials

(for finished size 18" × 47¾" [46cm × 121cm])

* Dark fabric: ⅔ yard (.6m) (total of about 20" [51cm])

* Light to medium focus fabric: ½ yard (.5m)

* Backing fabric: 1½ yard (1.4m)

* Quilt batting (very thin loft): 22" × 52" (56cm × 132cm)

* Binding*: 4½ yards (4m); can make your own from four 2½" (6cm) strips

* Optional: Quilt basting spray

* This tablerunner has ½" (12mm) binding.

Serger settings

* 3 or 4 thread overlock
* **Stitch length:** 2.5 to 3mm
* **Stitch width:** 6 to 8mm
* **Cutting blade:** ON
* **Differential feed:** Adjust as necessary
* **Foot:** Standard serger foot
* **Seams:** All are ½" (12mm)

1 Cut all quilt, backing and batting pieces.

From the dark fabric, cut:
- two 4" × 14¾" (10cm × 38cm) strips
- two 4" × 20" (10cm × 51cm) strips
- two 12" × 18" (31cm × 46cm) rectangles

From the focus fabric, cut:
- two 4" × 12" (10cm × 31cm) strips
- two 4" × 18" (10cm × 46cm) strips
- two 6" × 8" (15cm × 20cm) pieces

From the backing fabric, cut:
- two 4" × 12" (10cm × 31cm) strips
- two 4" × 14¾" (10cm × 38cm) strips
- two 4" × 18" (10cm × 46cm) strips
- two 4" × 20" (10cm × 51cm) strips
- two 6" × 8" (15cm × 20cm) pieces
- two 12" × 18" (31cm × 46cm) rectangles

From the batting, cut:
- two 4" × 12" (10cm × 31cm) strips
- two 4" × 14¾" (10cm × 38cm) strips
- two 4" × 18" (10cm × 46cm) strips
- two 4" × 20" (10cm × 51cm) strips
- two 6" × 8" (15cm × 20cm) pieces
- two 12" × 18" (31cm × 46cm) rectangles

2 Start with the two 6" × 8" (15cm × 20cm) center blocks. Place two 6" × 8" (15cm × 20cm) backing pieces together, with right sides together. Then layer one batting piece, one focus fabric right-side up, one focus fabric right-side down, and one batting piece. Serge along one 6" (15cm) side.

Quilting tips

✂ Place all the pieces together and position on the serger so very little fabric and batting are cut while serging.

✂ Always square up after adding each new piece. Use a ruler, rotary cutter and mat. Place the ruler along the layered edges and cut the excess fabric.

✂ Before adding another section finger press all seams, and pin in place. Another option is using quilt basting spray to secure the layers.

✂ When adding new pieces to the quilt, always work with the right side of the quilt facing up.

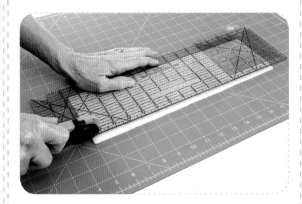

Squaring up.

3 Open the pieces so that the backing is on the bottom. Finger press the seam.

4 With the first unit right side up, place one 4" × 14¾" (10cm × 38cm) strip of backing underneath the unit, with the right side facing up. Then, on top of the first unit, place a 4" × 14¾" (10cm × 38cm) strip of dark fabric wrong side up. Place a 4" × 14¾" (10cm × 38cm) batting piece over that. Serge along the long edge. Open and finger press. Square up the edges.

5 Repeat for the other 4" × 14¾" (10cm × 38cm) side.

6 Repeat steps 4 and 5 using the 4" × 12" (10cm × 31cm) focus fabric, batting and backing.

7 Repeat steps 4 and 5 using the 4" × 20" (10cm × 51cm) dark fabric, batting and backing.

8 Repeat steps 4 and 5 using the 4" × 18" (10cm × 46cm) focus fabric, batting and backing.

9 Repeat steps 4 and 5 using the 12" × 18" (31cm × 46cm) dark rectangles, batting and backing.

10 Square up the final edges.

11 Head to your sewing machine and attach binding to the tablerunner to finish.

Layout diagram
F = focus fabric
D = dark fabric

(Diagram labels: D, F, F, F, D, D, F, F, F, D, D, F, F, D)

Add an appliqué

Have a large bare area on your tablerunner? Add an appliqué. Use the serger to stitch around the appliqué piece, adding an appearance of the blanket stitch. Then either hand sew or use your sewing machine to attach the appliqué to the tablerunner.

Serger tip

If one looper thread breaks, don't try to just rethread only the broken thread. Remember, the serger must be threaded in the proper sequence to sew properly. Check inside the looper cover, as the sequence may be visually shown.

Finished tablerunner

Serger Maintenance

Each time you use it, a serger gathers an enormous amount of lint, threads, and tiny bits of fabric that can become trapped around the loopers, knives and the feed dogs. Take a quick look inside your serger and see what might still be stuck among all the moving parts. You may be surprised at the amount! If you used your serger for several hours every day of the week (or more, like I do), you could have enough dust and fluff to stuff a small pillow!

One of the most valuable accessories that comes with your serger is the lint brush. Use it before, during and after all your projects. Allowing lint to build up can cause many stitch problems, along with bent needles and dull knives.

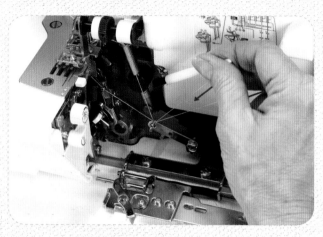

Continually brush away lint and dust to keep your serger working properly.

Cleaning and lubricating

Sergers create a lot of dust and lint, especially around the knives. They must be cleaned frequently, even several times during the same project. Use the lint brush regularly to keep your serger in good working order. I keep a small painter's brush tucked in the pocket of my thread catcher mat. Throughout a project, I continually clean away dust and fabric.

Most sergers need very little lubricating, and only in certain places. Only use sewing machine oil, as other types will be too heavy and may damage the machine. A good rule of thumb is to oil after every eight or nine hours of use. Read your manual to be sure you lubricate the right parts for your specific machine.

Cleaning tension disks

Lint builds up everywhere on a serger. To maintain perfect tension, don't forget to clean the tension disks. Tie three or four knots along a length of buttonhole twist thread, and soak it in a bit of alcohol. Work the thread back and forth between the disks.

Replacing needles

Dull and bent needles cause stitch problems, so check and change them often. If your serger stitch uses two needles, they must be the same size. Most sergers take regular household needles of system 130/705H. For regular applications, use sizes 70–90. Delicate cover stitch and chainstitch may fare better with JLx2 needles. Just as with a conventional sewing machine, needle size is matched to the fabric weight. Check your manual for any specific needle sizes and suggestions.

A very useful accessory is a needle inserter. Keep it nearby so needles can be inserted quickly and easily without undue eye strain. To replace, raise the needles. Turn the handwheel in the normal direction until fully raised. Using a small screwdriver from your accessory kit, loosen the needle setscrews and remove the needles. You may have one to three needles to replace. Make it a habit to change them all at the same time.

It is easier to insert the right-hand needle first, and then the left one(s). Insert the needle with the flat side toward the back, until it is in place as high as possible. Tighten the needle setscrew. Most importantly, insert the new needle into the same needle slot. Some sergers have up to five needle locations for the overlock, cover stitch, and the chainstitch.

Clean the tension disks by working a rubbing alcohol-soaked thread back and forth between them.

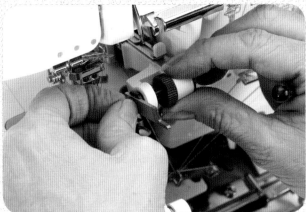

Raise the upper knife before replacing the lower knife.

Replacing knives

Having sharp upper and lower knives is critical to serging, as they cut the fabric right before stitching. A nice, clean cut gives the best finished stitch without leaving a jagged edge. The upper knife may need changed every one to five years, and the lower knife about every four to six months. Fabric affects the lifetime of the knives. Synthetics tend to dull them faster than cottons. A serger knife is not made to be sharpened, so always keep extra on hand.

It is important to always turn the serger off whenever changing either of the knives. If you are not sure how to change either of the knives, take the serger to your dealer and watch them change them (in fact, it's recommended that you always have them change the upper knife, rather than doing it yourself). Also, it is very important to check your manual for specific instructions for your machine. I give only general instructions here, and yours may differ in how to remove and replace the knives. It is very important to retain the factory alignment of both knives, so be careful with them. Purchase only knives that are specific to your machine. Again, if you have any uncertainty, take your serger to a service repairman.

Changing the upper knife

The upper knife is made of more durable steel than the lower knife, so it may not wear out as fast as the lower one. It is held on by a hex screw, and it is recommended that you have a service dealer replace it.

Changing the lower knife

To change the lower knife, fully raise the needles first. Raise the upper knife, and loosen the screw holding the lower knife on. Remove and replace the lower knife, making sure it is level with the stitch plate. Your machine may have a groove the knife inserts into. If so, make sure everything is lined up perfectly, then tighten the screw. Turn the handwheel so the two blades work together. Do this several times to remove any possible uneven parts of the new blade.

Glossary

Balanced stitch: A stitch that has been adjusted so the upper looper, lower looper and needle threads lock precisely together at the edge of the fabric.

Beading foot: Designed with a top groove to guide strings of pearls, beads, sequins, etc.

Bite: Another name for stitch width. Affects how much fabric is used to achieve the stitch.

Blades: A serger has two blades, upper and lower (also called knives). The blades cut the fabric right before stitching.

Blind hem: A technique that hems and finishes the edges in one step, using the blind hem serger foot. Stitches are nearly invisible on the right side of the fabric.

Chain looper: If your serger is capable of creating the chainstitch or cover stitch, it must have a chain looper. The chain looper moves below the fabric and interlocks with the looper threads.

Chain tail: *see* Thread tail

Chaining off: *see* Stitching off

Chainstitch: Produced when using only one needle and the chain looper. The top (needle side) looks like a sewing machine straight stitch, while the bottom (looper side) appears as a row of loops, or chain. Can be used for seams or decorative stitches.

Converter: A spring-type mechanism that fits into a small hole at the top of the upper looper. Once in place, the looper "thinks" it is threaded and can then be used for a specific stitch.

Cover stitch: A serger stitch that does not trim or overedge. The upper knife is disengaged. Has two or three parallel lines on the needle side, and underneath has loops between the rows of stitching. Created with two or three needles and one looper.

Cording foot: Designed with a bottom groove that guides the piping between two layers of fabric. Use with commercially prepared bias binding, or you can make your own.

Cross-wound thread: The thread is put on the spool or cone so that it crosses over itself diagonally as the spool is wound. Cross-wound thread pulls from the top.

Cutting width: Cutting width is the stitch width on a serger. Can be adjusted from 5–9mm ($\frac{3}{16}$"–$\frac{11}{32}$") on most machines. Seam width is measured from the left needle (if serger has two needles).

Differential feed: Two sets of feed dogs, one front and one rear. They move independently of each other, providing a stretch to the stitch. The distance each feed dog travels during one complete movement can be adjusted as necessary. This feature is available on some machines and can prevent puckering, or stretched seams. When set to a higher number, it gathers the fabric, but a lower number builds stretch into the seam.

Disengage the blade: Adjusting the blade so that it does not cut the fabric while serging. On some machines the blade is moved down and locked into position, while on others the blade is turned up and out of the way.

Elasticator foot: Designed to guide elastic and stabilizing tapes while keeping away from the knives.

Feed dogs: Work in conjunction with the needles, pushing fabric as stitches are made.

Finished edges: Serging along a raw edge to give a clean overcast finish.

Flat construction: Keeping the garment flat as long as possible, such as serging edges which will be seamed and later pressed open. It is always easier to sew flat pattern pieces.

Flatlock: A flatlock stitch has a looped thread on one side and "ladders" on the other. It is created by tightening the lower looper tension and loosening the needle tension for a 2-, 3- or 4-thread overlock. The seam is serged and then gently pulled apart, so serging becomes flat. Upper threads form the overlock stitch while the threads underneath form a ladder stitch. Can be used for seaming fabrics together and also for decorative purposes. Allows the fabric seam to lie flat, having the seam allowance encased in the stitches.

Gathering foot: The gathering foot gathers fabric while being serged. It also has the capability of gathering the fabric while being sewn to a second fabric.

Handwheel: The handwheel turns in a counter-clockwise direction on most sergers. It is located on the side of the serger. The handwheel cycles the cutting blades and can be used to manually raise and lower the needles.

Jet-air threading: Exclusive to Baby Lock sergers. A touch of a lever sends the thread through a tubular looper using a burst of air. This type of threading is used for the upper, lower and chain loopers.

Knife guard: Also called the serger plate. Many have seam guide markings.

Knives: The two blades in a serger that trim the fabric right before stitches are formed.

Ladders: The stitch formation on the underside of a flatlock stitch.

Looper cover: The door that covers the lower part of the serger, where the loopers are. On some machines, accessories may be stored inside the looper cover.

Looper threader: A looper threader is a tool with a long loop at one end. The thread is inserted through the loop and pulled back through the looper eye.

Loopers: The serger has two loopers, an upper and a lower, to create the overlock stitch. They carry the thread from side to side to create the thread loops that encase the edges of serged fabrics.

Mock safety stitch: Most often, the 4-thread stretch stitch sewn on a 4/3/2 thread serger. Some models may also have a 3-thread mock safety stitch.

Needle inserter: Helps to insert needles quickly and easily. Designed to grip each needle and hold securely in place while tightening the setscrew.

Nets: Mesh plastic nets used to cover serger comes and spools to present thread from coming off too fast or tangling around the spool. Especially helpful with slippery threads such as rayon or woolly nylon.

Overcast stitch: *see* Overedge

Overedge: A stitch that seams and finishes the edge of fabric to prevent raveling.

Overlock machine: Another name for a serger.

Overlock stitch: A stitch that locks together at the edge of a seam allowance. It both sews and finishes the seam.

Piping: Folded fabric strip with cord inside; adds interest and texture.

Piping foot: A serger foot with a groove underneath to slide cord into; helps it glide over the piping while being stitched in place. Allows you to create and attach piping in one step.

Pokies: Snips of fabric that stick out from a serged fabric edge.

Presser foot: Holds the fabric against the feed dogs while the stitches are formed.

Pressure control: Screw or a knob normally located on the top of a serger to increase or decrease the pressure of the presser foot while serging. Turn clockwise for more pressure, and counterclockwise for less. You will use less pressure on stretchy fabrics and more pressure on heavy fabrics.

Rolled edge hem: Also called the rolled edge stitch and the narrowest 2- or 3-thread stitch. The stitch rolls under the fabric edge and covers with thread. Use as decorative hem or to finish the edges on lightweight fabrics.

Safety stitch: An additional stitch that is sewn with one of the needle threads; the fourth thread of a 3/4-thread serger or the chainstitch in a 5- or 6-thread stitch.

Seam sealant: Used to seal thread ends to prevent unraveling.

Securing thread tails: To lock serger seams and prevent unraveling.

Serger: A machine that stitches, trims and overcasts seams in one step.

Setscrew: Screws holding the needles in place.

Spool cap: A spool cap is placed on top of a spool of thread to allow threads to wind off smoothly.

Spool pin: Located on the back of the serger for holding the needle and looper thread spools or cones.

Standard serger foot: Used during general construction. Holds fabric against the feed dogs while serging.

Stitch finger: The metal prong(s) on the needle plate or the presser foot. Stitches form around the stitch finger and the edge of the fabric at the same time.

Stitch length: The distance in millimeters between the needle thread and the trimmed edge of the fabric.

Stitch width: *see* Cutting width

Stitching off: At the end of serging a seam, continuing to stitch beyond the edge of the fabric.

Tail chain: *see* Thread tail

Tape guide: A groove in the standard serger foot that holds tape and ribbon in place while serging.

Tapestry needle: Has a large hole in one end and can be used to secure thread tails by weaving back into the stitching.

Telescopic rod: Metal rods at the back of the serger having the first open thread guide on it. The rod must always be in the raised position when sewing.

Tension: The pressure exerted on thread as it passes through the tension disks.

Tension dials: Tension dials are turned to maintain the proper amount of tension on needles and thread, achieving a balanced stitch. When the presser foot is raised, the tension is released.

Thread tail: A thread tail is created when you stitch beyond the fabric's edge.

Thread stand: Attached to and sitting on the back of the serger to hold the numerous spools or cones of thread. The telescopic rod is inserted into the thread stand.

Threading sequence: A serger has a proper sequence of threading to keep threads from becoming tangled. Follow this sequence as directed (see page 32).

Waste catcher: A plastic container that attaches to the front of the serger to collect excess fabric and threads as they are trimmed by the cutting knives.

Wrapped edge: Eliminates bulk when seams intersect (see page 42).

(see page 32).

(see page 42).

RESOURCES
SERGER COMPANIES

Baby Lock U.S.A.
www.babylock.com

BERNINA of America
www.berninausa.com

Brother International Corp.
www.brother.com

Elna USA
www.elnausa.com

Janome
www.janome.com

Juki
www.juki.com

Necchi/Allyn International
www.allynint.com

Pfaff
www.pfaff-us-cda.com

Singer Sewing Co.
www.singerco.com

Viking Sewing Machine Inc.
www.husqvarnaviking.com

Index

About the Author

Charlene Phillips is an author, magazine contributor, presenter and trainer. She lives in southwestern Ohio with her husband, Bryan. Together they own and operate The Sew Box, a store specializing in sewing machine feet, notions and self-designed sewing patterns. Since her mother taught her to sew at a very young age, Charlene has continued to learn and share sewing techniques with others, reaching "new sewing friends" around the world. More information can be found at www.thesewbox.com. Charlene enjoys hearing from others, and sharing tips through her blog at http://thesewbox.blogspot.com. Continual sewing conversation can be found by joining her on Facebook (The Sew Box).

Previously, Charlene owned an alterations business, was a school teacher, a college professor and an educational trainer for local schools. She is the author of *The Sewing Machine Classroom* and *The Sewing Machine Attachment Handbook*, and contributes to many magazines and online sites such as *Threads*, *Sew News*, *Creative Machine Embroidery* and *ISMACS News*. She is also a guest blogger for BERNINA of America's blog, WeAllSew (www.weallsew.com).

Charlene has presented and taught locally, as well as at various Quilt Markets and conferences.

Acknowledgments

There are so many people that are always behind me, supporting me and cheering me on. I would love to mention every single person by name, but that would be a book of its own.

Always at the top of my list, and the people I couldn't ever do without, is my family. I don't know how he does it, but my husband, Bryan, puts up with this sewist and never fails to support all my endeavors. He doesn't always understand what I am writing, but knows how to insert all those yesses and uh-huhs at the right time. My sons, Troy and Charles, and their lovely wives, Tracy and Carrie, totally enrich my life, which enriches my writing! A huge hug goes to my daughter, Shirley. She continually reminds me to take time for myself and is a true role model for me.

When you have four grandchildren, you never run out of things to sew—just time! Besides providing so many projects to keep me busy, they are all my heroes, continuously providing me with laughter and love. I am so proud of them! Thank you Chance, Corin, Maggie and Robbie. I am blessed.

I grew up with four siblings, yet Mom and Dad gave special time to us all, which was not an easy task at times. Virgia and Charles Smith (aka Mom and Dad), thank you for lessons learned—even the hard ones. Dolores Smith is not only a wonderful stepmother, but when my eyes glazed over just staring at the fabric surrounding me, she came up with some great ways to use some. To my siblings—Mike, Calvin, Joyce and Monica—all those shenanigans did help teach me to sew. I had to get out of the way somehow!

A big thank-you to Megan McGuire. You will see some samples of her work in the project section. She spends her days at Pohlar Fabrics in Liberty, Indiana, with her lovely mother and store owner, Rose. Thank you also to Mark of The Colorful World of Sewing for the extra serger feet. A heartfelt thanks to both BERNINA of America and Singer Sewing Co. for the lovely loaner machines.

A huge thanks to those who contributed questions about using a serger, which are sprinkled throughout the book. You are an inspiration to me!

This book was just words on paper until editors Kelly Biscopink and Stefanie Laufersweiler came along and worked editorial magic. They sorted out the technical details and found all those things that just didn't make sense. All the fabulous step-by-step photos are due to the photographic talent of Christine Polomsky. Ladies, every moment with you is always fulfilling—both for the stomach and the mind! Thanks also to Jack Kirby for the amazing shots of the finished projects. Thank you again, F+W Media, for surrounding me with fantastic nonstop talent.

Dedication

This book is dedicated to my sister Monica Helton—always my sewing buddy and one of those rare people with a great eye for color and combinations. To never give up and to live life to the fullest every day, with determination and zest, will be her lasting tribute. I will always be in awe of her strength.

Metric Conversion Chart

To convert	to	multiply by
Inches	Centimeters	2.54
Centimeters	Inches	0.4
Feet	Centimeters	30.5
Centimeters	Feet	0.03
Yards	Meters	0.9
Meters	Yards	1.1

Measurements have been given in imperial inches with metric conversions in parentheses. Use one or the other as they are not interchangeable. The most accurate results will be obtained using inches.

 www.fwmedia.com

media   16   15   14   13   12   5   4   3   2   1

DISTRIBUTED IN CANADA BY FRASER DIRECT
100 Armstrong Avenue
Georgetown, ON, Canada L7G 5S4
Tel: (905) 877-4411

DISTRIBUTED IN THE U.K. AND EUROPE BY F&W MEDIA INTERNATIONAL
Brunel House, Newton Abbot, Devon, TQ12 4PU, England
Tel: (+44) 1626 323200, Fax: (+44) 1626 323319
Email: enquiries@fwmedia.com

DISTRIBUTED IN AUSTRALIA BY CAPRICORN LINK
P.O. Box 704, S. Windsor NSW, 2756 Australia
Tel: (02) 4577-3555

ISBN-13: 978-1-4402-3021-9
ISBN-10: 1-4402-3021-8
SRN: W8607

Edited by Kelly Biscopink and Stefanie Laufersweiler
Designed by Charly Bailey
Production coordinated by Greg Nock
Photographed by Christine Polomsky and Jack Kirby

Connect — Inspire — Create

Join our online craft community for exclusive offers and daily doses of inspiration.

 fwcraft   @fwcraft

Watch an exclusive interview with *Simply Serging* author Charlene Phillips at http://www. marthapullen. com/simply- serging.html.

Ready, Set, Serge

Quick and Easy Projects You Can Make in Minutes

Georgie Melot

Learn the ins, outs, overs and unders of your serger! Explore the creative options with Georgie Melot's tried-and-true methods. Contains 16 basic projects for the home and and 16 "stepped-up" versions.

Serge With Confidence

100+ Tips, Techniques & Projects Anyone Can Do

Nancy Zieman

In this beginner's guide to serging, Nancy Zieman demonstrates the essential skills to quickly and easily create stunning fashions, accessories and home décor projects, more quickly than with a regular sewing machine. Inside you'll find guidelines to serging tools and terms, and 20 projects to enhance your home and wardrobe.